Purchasing Medical Innovation

Purchasing Medical Innovation

*The Right Technology, for the Right
Patient, at the Right Price*

James C. Robinson

UNIVERSITY OF CALIFORNIA PRESS

University of California Press, one of the most distinguished university presses in the United States, enriches lives around the world by advancing scholarship in the humanities, social sciences, and natural sciences. Its activities are supported by the UC Press Foundation and by philanthropic contributions from individuals and institutions. For more information, visit www.ucpress.edu.

University of California Press
Oakland, California

Library of Congress Cataloging-in-Publication Data

Robinson, James C. (James Claude), 1953– author.
    Purchasing medical innovation : the right technology, for the right patient, at the right price / James C. Robinson.
        pages   cm
    Includes bibliographical references and index.
    ISBN 978-0-520-28166-0 (cloth : alk. paper)
    ISBN 978-0-520-96081-7 (ebook)
    1. Medical technology—Cost control.   2. Medical innovations—Cost control.   3. Medical care, Cost of.   4. Medical care—Cost control.   5. Health care reform   6. Health insurance.   I. Title.
    R855.3.R63   2015
      610.28—dc23

                                        2014030642

Manufactured in the United States of America

24 23 22 21 20 19 18 17 16 15
10 9 8 7 6 5 4 3 2 1

In keeping with a commitment to support environmentally responsible and sustainable printing practices, UC Press has printed this book on Natures Natural, a fiber that contains 30% post-consumer waste and meets the minimum requirements of ANSI/NISO z39.48–1992 (R 1997) (*Permanence of Paper*).

CONTENTS

ILLUSTRATIONS

FIGURES

TABLES

ACKNOWLEDGMENTS

This book builds on several years of research conducted through the Berkeley Center for Health Technology (BCHT) at the University of California. Many individuals and organizations have supported the Center and this research, for which I am grateful. Kim MacPherson, BCHT Co-Director, was the original proponent and has been my personal and professional partner throughout this project. Tim Brown, fellow economist and Director of Research, and Peg Farrell, BCHT administrative manager, have been invaluable. Special help to the Center was provided in different ways by Colleen David, Krista Burris, Kristin Stewart, and Francis Megerlin. I am especially grateful for the contributions of the BCHT graduate student research assistants, including Emma Dolan, Richard Fessler, Marina Fisher, Chris Whaley, Jessica Gall, Deirdre Parsons, Vanessa Polk Kaul, Alexis Pozen, and Erika Heaton. Core support and collaboration for the Center and our research have come from a variety of individuals, including most importantly Kent Lieginger, Scott Howell, John Hernandez, Kevin Bozic, Brian O'Shea,

Corine Muegge, Steve Halasey, Jamie Caillouette, Kathy Donneson, and Tad Funahashi. Numerous health care organizations have provided logistical support and allowed themselves and their data to be studied, including Kaiser Permanente, St. Joseph Health, Genentech, Anthem Blue Cross, Tenet, MemorialCare Health Systems, Blue Shield of California, CalPERS, Hoag Orthopedic Institute, and Safeway. Funding for the Center has come most prominently from Genentech, the US Agency for Health Care Quality and Research, the Robert Wood Johnson Foundation, InHealth, and the California HealthCare Foundation. The origins of my research on purchasing and innovation in orthopedics and cardiology lie in work done with the Integrated HealthCare Association, supported by the Blue Shield of California Foundation and AHRQ. It has been great working with the IHA and its energetic staff, including Tom Williams, Jill Yegian, Wesley Kary, Kelly Miller, Dolores Yanaghara, Michelle Denatale, and Jett Stansbury.

Innovation in medical technology is the engine that drives the health care system. What can be done for patients today is radically different from what could be done ten or twenty years ago, to say nothing of what went under the name of medicine in earlier years. Tremendous progress has been made in the treatment of formerly intractable conditions such as arthritis, heart disease, breast cancer, spinal deformities, and multiple sclerosis. Severely diseased coronary valves can be replaced by artificial implants delivered surgically or by catheters threaded through the body's major arteries. Replacement of diseased joints is done quicker, more cheaply, and with fewer complications than in years past, allowing the procedure to be extended to patients who formerly were forced to endure their pain and limit their activities. And the benefits of innovation extend beyond the patients. Investments in product development create a virtuous cycle of new products, jobs, and revenues, followed by more research and another generation of technology. The life sciences are a pillar of the knowledge-based economy.

But innovation in medical technology is also the source of the unsustainable growth in health care expenditures. When Medicare was created in 1965, the United States spent $208 per person on health care, accounting for 5.7 percent of the nation's economic output. Over the following two decades, expenditures per person more than doubled, rising to 10.4 percent of total output. After another twenty years, by 2005, expenditures per person had doubled again. By the end of the decade, they had risen to over seventeen cents of every dollar spent in the nation. These increases were not due to deteriorating health and an increasing need for care; on the contrary, the US population enjoys longer and healthier lives than did previous generations. The dramatic increase in health care expenditures is due to the adoption of new medical technology, defined broadly to include new drugs, devices, diagnostics, and procedures, plus the facilities and staffing needed to administer them.

If new technology improves the quality but also increases the cost of health care, how is the nation to balance its budget without crimping and ultimately crippling the dynamic of innovation? Our health system often uses new technologies on the wrong patient, in the wrong manner, or at the wrong time. A fortunate by-product of this unfortunate state of affairs is that there exist numerous ways to moderate expenditures by reducing inappropriate uses of technology without interfering with the appropriate uses. Indeed, the only sustainable way to moderate cost growth without undermining innovation is to improve the process of assessing, purchasing, and using technology. This requires fundamental change. For too long the FDA has focused on evidence of technology performance conducted prior to market launch, to the neglect of performance under real-world conditions after launch. Medicare and private insurers have extended coverage to technologies without rigorous analysis of costs and comparative clinical effectiveness. Hospitals have competed for physicians by acquiring every new machine and for patients by offering every new amenity. Many patients have insisted on unnecessary treatments while others have neglected even the most effective forms of care.

In nonhealth sectors of the economy, the value of a good or service is defined in terms of what the consumer wants and is willing to pay for. Value in medical technology is more complicated, since the assessment of performance requires scientific expertise, while financial access to expensive tests and treatments requires insurance. Nevertheless, the same goals and rules apply. The purchasing of medical technology must change.

There are many reasons for optimism. The FDA is more thoroughly assessing product performance after as well as before market launch. Insurers are tightening coverage criteria and designing more incentive-conscious provider payment methods. Hospitals are developing more sophisticated methods of supply chain management. Patients are becoming more accountable for the selection and payment of their own care.

This book analyzes the purchasing of medical technology within a framework that includes the roles of the FDA, insurers, physicians, hospitals, and consumers themselves. The framework applies broadly to all forms of medical technology, but the book will illustrate it primarily with examples from the assessment, payment, and use of implantable medical devices such as artificial heart valves and joint replacements. The book analyzes the existing structure of technology purchasing and highlights ways in which it should be improved. The goal of the book is to help the buyers, sellers, and users to improve value: better performance at lower cost for medical technology.

A FIRST EXAMPLE:
ARTIFICIAL HEART VALVES

The clinical achievements and financial challenges raised by medical innovation are well illustrated by the evolution of treatment for severely diseased heart valves. Approximately half a million Americans, 3 percent of elderly persons over the age of seventy-five, suffer from aortic valve stenosis each year, and a third of these are candidates for an artificial valve. Valve replacement traditionally has been performed through open-heart surgery, a complex and risky procedure that can be used only on the healthiest patients. Until recently, patients with severe stenosis who were not candidates for surgery had no good alternative option, and three-quarters of them died within three years of diagnosis.

In the past decade cardiologists have developed catheter-based interventions that can dramatically improve the lives of patients too frail to be treated surgically, which are referred to as transcatheter aortic valve replacement (TAVR). By 2010, six firms were marketing TAVR devices in Europe and catheter-based procedures accounted for 20 percent of all valve replacements. There was active competition among new valve designs and methods of use. Numerous firms, both small and large, sought to enter the rapidly expanding market.[1] But, as of 2010, no TAVR product had been approved by the FDA for use in the United States. Why not?

The evolution of artificial heart valves raises important questions concerning the appropriate assessment and regulation of innovative technologies. Did the FDA err in waiting until 2011 to approve the first TAVR model for the US market, impeding access for American patients and disadvantaging American firms in global competition? Or, on the contrary, did the agency conduct a more thorough scientific review than its European counterparts and impose limits that ensured safe and effective use? How high should the bar be for access to the market, and what is the appropriate role for follow-on studies of how new technologies perform in the real world?

If we move beyond the FDA and initial permission to enter the market, how should TAVR be treated by Medicare and private health insurance plans? Should reimbursement be limited to large hospitals with dedicated catheter and surgical teams, or should the procedure diffuse widely? How should payment to physicians and hospitals be structured? Historically payments have been made on a fee-for-service basis to each physician and surgeon independently, with another complicated set of payments going to the hospital and the device manufacturer. This fragmentation of payment undermines coordination and efficiency. Is there a better way to pay for TAVR?

And what about the patient? Should the consumer pay a portion of the cost? Would cost sharing reduce demand for unnecessary procedures or, on the contrary, impede access to appropriate uses? How can patients be encouraged to share with physicians in the choice between surgical, TAVR, and drug treatment for their illness in ways that respect their values and preferences? Should they face incentives to consider price as well as the quality at competing hospitals?

A SECOND EXAMPLE:
ARTIFICIAL KNEES AND HIPS

TAVR is directed at elderly patients facing life-threatening cardiac disease, but many medical technologies are designed to improve the quality rather than the quantity of life. Arthritis is a chronic and progressive disease of the bones and joints that, over time, reduces mobility, inflicts increasing pain, and reduces the ability to perform the functions of daily life. The first line of defense against arthritis should be changes in lifestyle, including weight loss, and simple medical interventions, such as the use of anti-inflammatory drugs. However, arthritis tends to progress with time, regardless of preventive efforts, and has grown in prevalence as the population has aged. The loss of mobility has increased in prominence as many seniors have pursued more active lifestyles than earlier generations.

Over the past several decades, orthopedic surgeons have worked with device manufacturers to develop artificial implants that can replace severely arthritic joints. The prostheses combine metal, plastic, and ceramic and are implanted after the surgical removal of the original joint. Most patients experience a remarkable reduction in pain and a renewed ability to walk and work. Some return to jogging or even competitive running. The combination of an aging population, increased cultural emphasis on function, and ever-improving technology performance has dramatically expanded the demand for artificial joints. Between 2005 and 2010, the number of Americans receiving artificial hips increased from 232,000 to 293,000, while the number receiving artificial knees grew from 471,000 to 650,000. These numbers are expected to grow to over 500,000 and 1.4 million, respectively, by 2020.[2]

Surgical joint replacement is a modern medical miracle, but it collides head-on with the FDA approach to regulating the safety and efficacy of new technologies. The gold standard of FDA review is the randomized clinical trial, a lengthy and expensive research endeavor in which patients are selected at random to receive the new intervention or, alternatively, to be treated with conventional therapies. The randomized trial works well for major new technologies, such as pharmaceutical molecules or cardiac defibrillators. But orthopedic implants improve incrementally, with each generation modestly modifying previous versions. Most models only have a few years of effective market value before they are surpassed. One cannot spend three years studying a new device that will only be used for one year. And how can we conduct randomized clinical trials for these highly visible interventions? Patients have strong preferences for or against surgery, and often will be unwilling to be used as guinea pigs.

Joint replacements also raise thorny problems for health insurers. The first candidates for surgery are typically patients with moderate disease who have the best chance of improvement. But once a procedure is established, it tends to spread to frail patients at risk for major complications and, conversely, to patients with only moderate disease who should rely on medications and lifestyle changes. The clinical evidence always is collected for patients with the best prognosis, but then the procedure tends to experience "indication creep" to a wider population. This is an even greater concern for spine surgery, where the underlying causes of pain are poorly understood, the procedures are less effective, and the potential profits to surgeons and device manufacturers are greater than for joint replacement. Which uses of orthopedic surgery should be covered by insurance? How can health plans encourage a procedure for some patients while discouraging it for others? Should they even try?

The costs and quality of joint replacement depend not only on the procedure and the implant, but on the patient's entire course of care. How should payments be structured for the radiology done prior to hospital admission, and for the physical therapy done after discharge? Should the hospital be paid more if the patient has a long length of stay, perhaps due to a surgical complication? What about if the patient is readmitted after an infection that develops at home? Separate fee-for-service payment for each test, intervention, implant, and therapist seems illogical, but can payment be bundled to cover the entire care episode?

Joint replacements occur mostly in the hospital, though some now are being conducted on an ambulatory basis, and the implantable devices constitute an expensive part of the hospital's supply chain. How should hospitals assess device performance, as a first step toward deciding which to use and how much to pay? How can the often-divergent interests of physicians and hospitals be aligned so as to permit effective purchasing and appropriate use?

And again, what should be the role of the consumer? Manufacturers tout the higher-priced models using financial inducements to surgeons and glossy advertising to patients, even though research studies often find no differences in clinical outcomes. Should patients be required to pay part of the price of the more expensive models? What if the more expensive models do offer better quality? The rate of surgery could be reduced if disease management programs were more popular among patients. How can we engage consumers in their own health and health care?

THE FRAMEWORK OF VALUE-BASED PURCHASING

The clinical outcomes and economic costs of a medical technology depend on how it is used, where it is used, and on whom it is used. The efficacy of a drug is enhanced when it is prescribed for the appropriate indication, administered as part of an evidence-based protocol, and monitored for its impact on each individual patient. The value of diagnostic imaging and laboratory tests depends on appropriate timing in the course of a patient's illness and on whether the test results will influence choice of treatment. The benefits and costs of an implantable device depend on the skill of the surgeon, the efficiency of the hospital's service line, and the patient's own engagement in preparing for and recovering from the procedure.

The effectiveness of medical technology is not fixed at the time of initial market launch but often improves based on experience. Physicians learn to target drugs at the patients most likely to respond and to administer them in more effective combinations and doses. Diagnostic imaging becomes cheaper, faster, and more precise as it incorporates advances in electrical engineering and information processing. Implantable devices are subject to continual modifications in design, scale, materials, and methods of administration.

The purchasing of a medical technology cannot be a one-time event. Technology assessment builds on randomized clinical trials but includes follow-on studies, data on real-world uses, and analysis of how outcomes vary for particular providers and patients. The price for a technology is established initially by the manufacturer but then must be negotiated with insurers as part of coverage decisions and with hospitals as part of supply chain management. Patients make their own assessment of whether the expected benefits outweigh the cost sharing that is required.

An effective purchasing framework has four stages that build upon one another, in the sense that a test or treatment needs to pass the first stage before being considered for the second, the second before the third, and the third before the fourth. The four stages can be denoted regulatory market access, insurance coverage, care delivery, and patient engagement. A new technology must successfully demonstrate its safety and efficacy to the FDA, its clinical and cost effectiveness to health insurers, its value

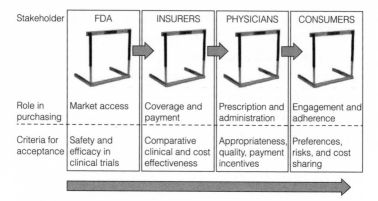

Stakeholder	FDA	INSURERS	PHYSICIANS	CONSUMERS
Role in purchasing	Market access	Coverage and payment	Prescription and administration	Engagement and adherence
Criteria for acceptance	Safety and efficacy in clinical trials	Comparative clinical and cost effectiveness	Appropriateness, quality, payment incentives	Preferences, risks, and cost sharing

Figure 1. Overcoming the hurdles to health care innovation: from the laboratory to the patient.

within the financial realities of the hospital's budget, and its bene-fits as interpreted by the patient. Each stage should contribute to the health care system's ability to foster innovation while dis-couraging ineffective treatment.

The framework of value-based purchasing is presented in figure 1. Let us summarize here how each stage is designed and should be redesigned; the book will develop the analysis in depth.

REGULATORY ACCESS TO THE MARKET

The purchasing of technology begins with the assessment of prod-uct safety and efficacy in research laboratories and clinical trials. In the research context the therapy is administered by specially trained physicians, with the appropriate selection and informed consent of patients, and in compliance with evidence-based proto-cols. The question being addressed is whether the diagnostic test is accurate, the drug is biologically active, and the device improves functional ability under ideal conditions. The question is not how the product performs when used under real-world conditions, where sometimes it is administered at the wrong time or dose, in the wrong setting, or without informed cooperation by the patient. The question is not whether the product creates better outcomes than alternative treatments or whether the health benefits exceed the economic costs. Those questions come later.

The mission of the FDA is to protect consumers by preventing market access for unsafe and ineffective medical products. The agency's challenge has been to decide how to balance this mission with the goal of supporting innovation. Even the most effective drugs are toxic at some doses and even the best-designed devices are harmful in the hands of poorly trained practitioners. No therapy works well when used on patients who do not suffer from the relevant disease or disability. But if the FDA rejected every product that creates any risk in any use, it would allow nothing onto the market. The agency must specify how much evidence is needed for market access, recognizing that weak criteria endanger patients while strong criteria impede innovation. The FDA also seeks to mitigate the regulatory burden it places on new technologies. It stratifies drugs and devices by potential risk, and sets a higher regulatory bar for those likely to impose irreversible harm. Similarly, it stratifies products by potential benefit, accelerating the review of breakthrough products that improve outcomes for patients suffering from previously intractable problems.

The FDA is hampered by the incompleteness of the available data at the time of product launch, as it is forced to approve or disapprove products without understanding their long-term impacts. It can raise the bar for market access, increasing its demands for studies that involve large and diverse populations, multiple clinical endpoints, and long follow-up periods. More studies reduce the chance that unsafe and ineffective products will gain access to the market, and thereby strengthen patient protection. But they add to the delays in access for patients with severe health problems, and contribute mightily to the cost of product development. Regulatory delays and costs contribute, in turn, to the ever-higher prices of new tests and treatments. High barriers lead developers to abandon some products altogether. Product prototypes that are denied access to the market never have the chance to improve.

The agency is modifying its emphasis on regulation of initial market access to include more assessment and surveillance after launch. This evolution is to be encouraged. Assessment of performance cannot be done definitively in research settings, as they differ so much from real-world conditions. Many risks and benefits only become evident over time and when the product is used on populations too large and diverse to be included in premarket studies. Observational studies based on electronic medical records and data registries provide essential complements to the traditional emphasis on randomized trials. Most importantly, the performance of a product cannot be separated from the manner in which it is used. Products that pose unacceptable risks to some patients or in some settings can offer important benefits to other patients or in other settings. Much innovation is incremental in nature, with many breakthrough products building on prototypes and precursors. Whenever possible, first-generation models should be allowed to improve through experience and experimentation.

INSURERS AS PURCHASERS

The second stage of technology purchasing is insurance coverage and reimbursement. Consumers have the right to spend their own money on their own care, but public and private insurers have a fiduciary duty to manage the resources of the community carefully. Proof of safety and efficacy in research studies, as demanded for FDA authorization, is necessary but not sufficient. Many technologies are not well integrated with the patient's course of care, are provided in unnecessarily costly facilities, or do not need to be used at all. For many years, however, insurers' coverage policies have erred on the side of inclusiveness. Medicare covers treatments deemed "reasonable and necessary," a vague term that has often been taken to imply any treatment prescribed by any physician for any patient. The agency lacks clear authority to employ comparative effectiveness research and has been prohibited from using cost effectiveness analysis for most coverage decisions. Private insurers have followed Medicare in extending coverage without regard to costs and comparative effectiveness.

Laxity in insurance coverage policy is not without its advantages, since even technologies that are frequently used in inappropriate ways can provide important benefits if targeted carefully. Indeed, the real question should not be whether a new medical technology is more effective or cost effective than an alternative treatment. Rather, the question should focus on comparative clinical and cost performance for particular patients in particular settings. Inclusive approaches to new technologies promote social value so long as they limit coverage to the contexts where they perform better than alternatives and where their benefits exceed their costs. This is the role of utilization and medical management.

Medical management programs require physicians and hospitals to obtain authorization prior to administering a treatment to a particular patient or, alternatively, require that the treatment be used as part of an evidence-based course of care. In principle, these programs prevent the use of drugs for inappropriate indications, reduce duplication of radiological tests, and favor outpatient over inpatient settings. In practice, unfortunately, these programs often impede the adoption of effective technologies. Medical management increases administrative burdens, envenoms relationships between insurers and providers, and has generated a regulatory backlash.

Rather than second-guess medical decisions, insurers should delegate to physicians the responsibility for appropriate use of medical technology. This is best done through payment methods that reward conservative rather than aggressive use. Traditional fee for service reimburses good and bad products without differentiation, while some of the emerging methods, such as case rates and population-based payment, reward coordinated and efficient care. But we must reform payments carefully, lest new methods discourage physicians from prescribing expensive technologies. Payments need to be adjusted for changes in technology over time, rising when costly innovations emerge and then falling as cheaper alternatives become available.

Insurers can and should supplement value-based payment methods with a selective approach to deciding which physicians and hospitals will be reimbursed for providing complex treatments. In markets with many providers, insurers can reduce costs by contracting with providers on the basis of price as well as outcomes. Selective networks channel more volume to hospitals that document their quality and discount their price, creating a market reward for efficiency.

HOSPITALS AS PURCHASERS

Hospitals purchase imaging equipment, laboratory tests, infused drugs, and implantable devices. Historically, they often used these technologies as a means to compete for physician affiliations and patient admissions. If one hospital acquired a new piece of equipment or created a new clinical facility, nearby hospitals would do likewise. This follow-the-leader pattern fostered excessive diffusion and undermined the regionalization of technology into Centers of Excellence. In most industries, competition leads to greater efficiency and lower costs, but in health care it led to lower efficiency and higher costs.

The medical arms race has been particularly vigorous for diagnostic and therapeutic technologies used in orthopedic surgery and interventional cardiology, two highly profitable hospital service lines. All the incentives have favored adoption and use. Physician would select medical devices based on their perceptions of quality, which often were based on limited personal experience and vigorous marketing by manufacturers, rather than the published evidence. Manufacturers cemented physician loyalty by paying honoraria linked to consulting, medical education, and other legitimate activities, but also implicitly linked to continued use of the newest and most expensive models. Hospitals were unwilling to antagonize physicians out of fear of losing patient admissions, and passed the costs of unneeded and overpriced technology on to insurers through higher charges.

This now is changing. Medicare pays hospitals through a prospective rate that includes all inputs, preventing carve-outs for implantable devices and other technologies. It is developing "shared savings" payment methods that reward physicians who manage the total cost of care, including hospitalization and ambulatory services. Private insurers are experimenting with episode-of-care and capitation methods in pursuit of the same goals.

Hospitals are responding to the changing environment by aligning more closely with their medical staffs and expanding their organizational capabilities. Leading institutions are developing technology assessment committees whose approval is a prerequisite for the adoption of new supplies and devices. They are reducing the number of manufacturers with whom they contract, obtaining volume-related price discounts and reducing the complexity of their inventory and staff training processes.

Technology firms are recognizing that their customer is now the hospital, aligned with its medical staff, rather than the individual physician. No longer will sales be made in the operating room or on the golf course. Sales will be made through the technology assessment committee and the supply chain staff, and will require evidence of superior performance or a willingness to discount prices. The transformation of the hospital is perhaps the single most important contemporary development in the market for medical technology. For too long the US health care system developed sophisticated technologies but used them in unsophisticated settings. Now, integrated physician and hospital organizations favor technology suppliers that offer the best products, and push them to improve the value of their services.

THE PATIENT AS PURCHASER

The fourth stage of the purchasing process comprises patients' decisions with respect to their own health care. Medical technologies are most effective when patients are educated and engaged, share with their doctors in clinical decision-making, take price as well as performance into account, and adhere to the chosen treatment regimen.

There has been a trend toward increased consumer cost sharing in health insurance, as employers and individuals seek to reduce the growth in premiums. Cost sharing motivates patients to think twice about whether they need a test or treatment and, if they do, to seek the most economical provider. We all spend our own money more carefully than we spend the money of others. Cost sharing can also foster a constituency for cost-conscious insurance coverage policy. Without cost sharing, consumers act as if health care financing were someone else's problem, and resist cost-reducing initiatives by their employers, their insurers, and the government.

While consumer cost sharing can improve value, it faces important limitations. Cost-sharing requirements are very complex and the patient often cannot understand his or her financial exposure before a service is chosen. Cost sharing varies among medical services without any guiding logic. There is too much required for effective therapies and not enough required for ineffective ones. Patient adherence is deplorably low for many important drugs, in part due to cost sharing, at a time when many well-insured consumers are overmedicating themselves against the normal challenges of daily life.

IMPLICATIONS FOR THE MEDICAL TECHNOLOGY INDUSTRY

For developers and manufacturers of medical technology, the US health care system has been a field of dreams. The FDA has promoted product innovation as well as consumer protection. Insurers have maintained broad criteria for coverage and reimbursement. Hospitals have competed to offer the most exotic technologies, and payment methods have rewarded increases in the volume of care. Patients have been protected by insurance and have demanded access to the newest treatments without regard to price.

The era of unsophisticated and cost-unconscious demand is coming to an end. The FDA is tightening its approval criteria for new therapies and mandating postapproval surveillance. Insurers are including comparative effectiveness in their coverage criteria and experimenting with payment methods that reward efficient delivery. Physicians and hospitals are developing more sophisticated mechanisms for the assessment, procurement, and use of technology. Patients are becoming more informed and engaged, but also are paying more out of their own pockets.

In the field of dreams, technology firms were able to pursue scientific opportunities and then look to society to cover the costs. Now they must orient their research toward the treatments most valued by purchasers. The important questions relate to market access, insurance coverage, hospital procurement, and patient engagement. Who are the most important buyers? What do they want and how much are they willing to pay? How will provider payment and consumer cost sharing influence choices? How can medical innovation be designed, financed, and promoted? What is value-based purchasing?

Regulatory Access to the Market

Patients want therapies that are safe and effective, yet the nation has all too much experience with treatments that poison the patient and with nostrums that do nothing at all. The US Food and Drug Administration (FDA) was established originally to protect consumers from tainted foods, but has seen its scope of authority expand to encompass pharmaceuticals, biologics, implantable devices, laboratory tests, diagnostic imaging, and radiation therapy. New products must obtain authorization from the agency prior to being made available for sale. The FDA's product label specifies the clinical indications for which the product can be marketed to physicians and, in some cases, requires the manufacturer to support a program of risk surveillance after the product is launched.

The FDA is not usually considered to be a purchaser of health care, as the agency neither pays for the products it regulates nor insures patients against the costs. In practice, however, the FDA performs two key purchasing functions. Through its regulatory requirements the agency generates most of the performance data that subsequently are used by those who do pay for medical technology. Furthermore, the agency's authority over market access frames the purchasing decisions of others. Insurers typically will not reimburse, physicians will not prescribe, and patients will not accept products that fail to achieve FDA approval for at least some uses, and the downstream purchasers often are skeptical regarding product uses that fall outside the FDA-approved indications.

It is essential that the FDA mandate rigorous testing for safety and efficacy, as many once-promising drugs and devices have proved to be ineffective against their intended targets. Others are so toxic that they should not be prescribed for any purpose. Some laboratory assays and imaging tests impair rather than improve the physician's ability to diagnose a disease. But ensuring safety and efficacy is not a simple task, and the FDA is besieged by critics who accuse it of doing too little, or, on the contrary, of doing too much.

The agency is now seeking a balance between premarket testing and access restrictions, on the one hand, and postmarket surveillance and risk mitigation, on the other. Many treatments are dangerous when used inappropriately but offer important benefits when used for the right indications, in the right setting, and in the right manner. Denying access to these products does not protect patients, but hurts them. It also short-circuits the possibility that the product or its method of use could improve over time. This is especially important for technologies that undergo frequent improvements based on experience, such as implantable medical devices. Postmarket surveillance also can strengthen consumer protection, since many treatments are found over time to pose greater risks than were evident at the time of initial approval. The shift in emphasis from premarket to postmarket surveillance needs to be accompanied by stronger regulatory controls on the manner of use, if risks are identified, and a strengthened ability to rescind market access if the risks prove unacceptable.

This chapter describes the role of the FDA as the first stage in the purchasing of medical technology. It begins with an overview of the agency's requirements for safety and efficacy as a condition for market access. It then considers the regulatory framework for implantable medical devices, which differs in important ways from the framework for drugs. The claim that the FDA fails to adequately protect patients is examined using the example of metal-on-metal hip implants, an initially promising product approved under the FDA's lenient standards for incremental innovation. The claim that the FDA imposes excessive regulatory burdens is considered using the example of aortic valve replacement, a breakthrough innovation that gained market access in Europe years before being approved by the FDA. The final section analyzes the FDA's balancing act between premarket authorization and postlaunch surveillance of medical technology.

PREMARKET TESTING AND AUTHORIZATION

The FDA has the statutory authority to deny market access to any product that has not proved itself safe and effective. Overcoming this regulatory hurtle does not guarantee, of course, that a new product will be reimbursed by insurers, prescribed by physicians, or embraced by patients. But failure to achieve FDA authorization for at least some purposes usually guarantees that it will not. And market access always is conditional, not absolute. Authorization can be retracted if the product is found to be significantly less effective or more dangerous than previously thought.

The primary mission of the FDA is consumer protection, but the agency cannot insist on complete safety. Every treatment poses at least some risk to some patients, at some doses, or in some settings. The acceptability of risk can only be assessed relative to the benefits offered. The FDA therefore requires proof of efficacy as well as safety. A new test must accurately identify the targeted trait, symptom, or condition, while a new treatment must alleviate the targeted disability or disease. Therapies that raise concerns may still receive authorization if no safer alternatives are available. Chemotherapies that target cancer, for example, often cause nausea, pain, and other serious side effects. They receive FDA authorization due to the life-threatening nature of the illness. The agency is less tolerant of toxic treatments for milder conditions. It was willing to withdraw market authorization for anti-inflammatory drugs that caused side effects in a small fraction of patients, for example, because safer and equally effective products were available.

The FDA's regulatory requirements add substantially to the time needed to get medical technology to market, cutting deeply into potential sales and revenues. Most tests and treatments are protected by patents and cannot legally be replicated for twenty years. But patents are filed early in the research and development process, and the product's twenty years of protection are often half over before it obtains FDA approval.[1]

Drugs spend the first few years of the patent protection period undergoing laboratory assays and animal studies. The bigger delays come with the three phases of clinical trials in humans. A promising treatment is first used on a small number of healthy volunteers to ascertain toxicity and seek a threshold for safety. The second phase of clinical trials uses patients who suffer from the disease of interest, and seeks evidence on efficacy as well as additional insight into adverse side effects. These two phases often add four years of delay to the hoped-for product launch.

The third phase of testing compares the impact of the new treatment with that of a placebo or a traditional form of care, using patients who have been assigned randomly to treatment and control groups. Randomization eliminates the confounding effect of unobserved patient characteristics. Large numbers of patients are important to give the study the statistical power to detect subtle impacts and to examine differences across patient subgroups. The length of the trial is often determined by the choice of treatment endpoint. The third phase of clinical testing usually adds another two to three years to the time until product launch.

Demands for more studies, covering more patients and with longer follow-up, have added immensely to the cost of medical innovation. Clinical trials are costly because physicians need to be engaged, patients recruited, the product contributed without reimbursement, study findings assessed, and an evidence dossier assembled. It costs an average of $1 billion to develop a new drug and get it successfully through FDA review.[2] The FDA has targeted regulatory delays and has made significant improvements with additional staffing from industry-supported fees on drug and device applications. Review times have decreased and approval rates increased.[3]

Once the drug or device patent expires, follow-on products jump into the market. Generic drugs, biopharmaceutical "similars," and follow-on devices are held to weaker standards of evidence than their reference products. This allows them to charge lower prices. Generic drugs are often priced at an 80 percent discount from the original brand, and follow-on biologics will be priced at a 25 percent discount.[4] Device prices usually decline over time.[5] This competition is good for the purchaser but bad for the innovator, who must match the competitor's price cuts or face substantial loss of sales.

Treatments are authorized by the FDA for some conditions, as described in the product label, but not for others. Product developers can only market their products to physicians for these approved indications. But physicians have the right to prescribe the product for indications outside the FDA label if they believe it will benefit their patients. These "off-label" uses are not necessarily inappropriate, since it is not possible for manufacturers to test and for the FDA to evaluate every therapy for every condition. But the FDA label remains the foundation for efforts to ensure appropriate use. Medical management programs developed by insurers, clinical protocols developed by professional societies, and informed consent programs developed for patients build on the label.

The FDA does not review evidence on the economic impact of the treatments that come under its purview. Some critics feel the agency should interpret its mission as promoting the value of health care, meaning that it should assess price as well as performance. Others counter that inclusion of cost analyses would further politicize an already-volatile regulatory process. The American public resists suggestions that access be denied if costs exceed a defined threshold. And even nations more comfortable with prioritizing medical expenditures situate cost analyses as part of insurance coverage policy, keeping the regulation of initial market access focused on health risks and benefits. That is a sensible principle.

THE REGULATION OF IMPLANTABLE MEDICAL DEVICES

The regulatory structure at the FDA was originally developed for drugs, but was extended to implantable medical devices in

1976 as innovation brought increased risks as well as benefits from those products. The FDA developed a three-part classification scheme that links the stringency of regulation to the characteristics of each device.[6] Devices that are life sustaining or pose significant risks, such as cardiac pacemakers and artificial valves, are required to go through the premarket approval (PMA) pathway. Intermediate-risk devices, such as imaging equipment and many orthopedic devices, do not need to prove safety and efficacy but are cleared through the more lenient 510(k) pathway after documenting "substantial equivalence" to an already-cleared predicate. Manufacturers of low-risk devices, such as hearing aids and prescription eyeglasses, do not need regulatory approval but merely notify the FDA prior to marketing their products.

The device sector is characterized by many incremental modifications of existing products, punctuated occasionally by an innovation that offers a significantly new mechanism of action, design, or risk profile. The FDA cannot require each variant of an evolving device to go through full premarket review. By the time the clinical trials were complete, the product would be outdated, and manufacturers might be discouraged from improving their product in the first place. Randomized trials are especially difficult to implement. It is difficult to sustain the confidentiality as to which patients have been assigned to the treatment and which to the control group, since devices involve surgery, catheterization, or another invasive procedure. Some patients resist randomization and insist on being in the treatment group. Others may acquiesce in their initial assignment but then insist on switching midway through the clinical trial. In the major clinical trial of spine fusion, for example, half of the patients assigned to surgery decided not to undergo the procedure while a third of the patients assigned to drug therapy decided they wanted the surgery.[7]

Full premarket approval is required only rarely for medical devices. Between 2003 and 2007, only 1 percent of the 15,000 new medical devices reviewed by the FDA went through the PMA pathway.[8] The agency appeared to set a lower bar for devices than for drugs, even for those going through the PMA pathway.[9] Only 1 percent of the devices going through PMA were denied approval. And, in fact, the majority of the regulatory actions for high-risk devices were not treated as new reviews but as supplements to earlier reviews. Between 2003 and 2007, the FDA authorized 170 original PMA applications but a total of 664 PMA supplements.[10] Supplements may include major or minor modifications in device structure as well as routine changes in labeling, materials, or manufacturing processes. Firms applying for a PMA supplement do not need to provide data on product safety and efficacy.

The importance of PMA supplements compared to original reviews is illustrated in the evolution of cardiac rhythm management devices such as pacemakers, defibrillators, and cardiac synchronization therapy.[11] Between 1979 and 2012, the FDA approved 77 original PMA applications for these devices, but also 5,829 supplement applications. Half of the supplemental applications concerned changes in manufacturing techniques and half concerned changes in design or materials. Of the supplements reporting a significant change in design or label, 23 percent mentioned the collection of new clinical data, but none involved randomized clinical trials. The heavy reliance on supplemental applications significantly reduces the delay and cost of FDA review, compared to what is required for an original PMA. However, the supplement process permits incremental changes to be made without clinical data even if the changes cumulatively transform the device. For example, one type of defibrillator lead wire that the FDA recalled from the market in 2011 due to serious adverse effects had undergone 78 supplemental applications and modifications since its original PMA review in 1996.[12]

For intermediate-risk devices, the FDA relies on comparisons with devices that are already in use, through what is referred to as the 510(k) premarket notification pathway. The 510(k) pathway is based on the concept that new devices equivalent to established devices in their structure and function are also equivalent in their risks and benefits. One-third of new devices are cleared for marketing through the 510(k) pathway.[13] The FDA has the authority to demand clinical data from these products, but rarely does so. Between 2005 and 2007, only 8 percent of the products submitted for 510(k) clearance contained data on safety and effectiveness, and only 11 percent of the predicate devices that they were judged as equivalent to had submitted such data.[14]

The principle of substantial equivalence is appropriate for devices that are subject to continual modification and have short shelf lives, but its application has often been inappropriate. A finding by the FDA that a new device is substantially equivalent to one on the market does not imply that the new device is safe and effective. Most established devices that are referenced in 510(k) submissions are new versions of devices that themselves never documented safety and efficacy. Rather, the predicate devices were cleared for marketing by the FDA as equivalent to an earlier product, which had been deemed equivalent to an even earlier one. Many predicate chains extend back to devices that were on the market prior to the original 1976 device legislation, and hence never passed any clinical review.

The principle of substantial equivalence has also been misused to permit the marketing of devices that the FDA classifies as posing significant risks. The 1976 legislation permitted use of the 510(k) pathway as a temporary expedient for high-risk devices that were already on the market, with the intention of having the agency subsequently review them through a full PMA process. But as of 2011, twenty-six classes of high-risk devices still had not completed PMA review and authorization.[15]

The FDA's principle of substantial equivalence is valid if it is applied judiciously, since many new devices can be expected to perform similarly to those they modify. Indeed, some variant of the principle is unavoidable. The PMA pathway cannot be used for every modification of every device, or the current generation of designs will be frozen in place. Ideally, the FDA builds on the 510(k) clearance process with a vigorous postmarket surveillance system.[16] But the agency is limited in its ability to intervene in how products are used once they have been cleared for market access. The agency has bolstered its postmarket risk management programs in recent years, but it is unclear whether these will remedy the shortcomings of the premarket 510(k) process.

CONSTRAINTS ON THE FDA

Weaknesses in FDA regulatory review stem in part from resource constraints on the agency. An internal FDA review of its regulatory process found insufficient staff, poor training, and high turnover. It also found that the data requirements imposed on manufacturers were excessive and inconsistent. For its part, industry contributed to the regulatory delay by submitting poor-quality clinical studies and incomplete applications.[17] The

2002 medical device legislation increased funding for the agency through fees imposed on firms submitting products for review. Unfortunately, regulatory delays grew worse and the rate of product approval declined in the following decade. The time required for a device to go through PMA review increased from 10.5 to 15.2 months, while the percentage of products authorized for market access declined from 90 percent to 59 percent. Similar regulatory problems beset the 510(k) pathway. Between 2005 and 2010 the number of 510(k) cases pending more than ninety days increased from sixty-nine to 119 and the average time to obtain clearance increased from three to five months.

In 2011 the FDA initiated a regulatory overhaul to reduce review times for both PMA and 510(k) applications.[18] The agency offered guidance to developers on how to design clinical studies, target the patients most likely to benefit, ensure safe methods of use, and monitor product performance. It prioritized products that target severe diseases and for which no safe treatments were already available. Some progress was achieved. Premarket review times for high-risk devices leveled off after 2010 and in the next two years showed a modest decline. The percentage of device reviews that obtained PMA authorization rose to 70 percent in 2012. During this period both the number of 510(k) cases under review and the number pending more than ninety days declined.

UNDERREGULATION? METAL–ON–METAL ARTIFICIAL HIPS

The challenge for FDA review created by incremental innovation has been illustrated forcefully in the case of the metal-on-metal artificial hip implant. The replacement of hips diseased by osteoarthritis has been one of the most impressive contributions of orthopedic surgery in recent decades, permitting many patients to regain mobility and resume normal lives. We now are accustomed to seeing senior citizens strolling and jogging when once they were confined to their homes or to a wheelchair. Surgeons excise the diseased head of the thighbone and replace it and its pelvic bone socket with high-performance metal, ceramic, and plastic implants. Outcomes have improved and costs have declined over time, leading to diffusion of the procedure to patients who previously would have been considered too frail or, conversely, too healthy to require surgery. By 2009 over a quarter million patients were receiving a hip replacement each year in the United States.[19] This is modern surgery at its best.

Hip replacement implants have been subject to continuous modification, with numerous changes in designs, materials, and methods of administration. Engineers experimented with metal-on-metal models, among other options, hoping to extend product utility and delay the revision surgeries that are often needed as the original implant ages. Surgeons experimented with partial replacement procedures, where only the thighbone but not the pelvic socket is removed, in order to leave the patient with as much natural bone as possible. Partial replacement techniques and metal-on-metal designs came together in the Articular Surface Replacement (ASR) product.

The ASR was approved for sale in Europe in 2003 based on simulation studies of how it would perform, but without clinical data on safety or effectiveness.[20] In 2005 the FDA classified the ASR hip implant as a high-risk device but cleared it through the 510(k) pathway as substantially equivalent to existing products. The manufacturer did not claim the ASR's equivalence to any single predicate but, rather, compared components of the ASR with components of various other implants, some of which had already been removed from the market.[21] The resurfacing and partial replacement technique for the ASR was never approved, but surgeons were able to use it outside the FDA label, since the device had been cleared for total joint replacement procedures. By 2010, thirty-seven thousand ASR hips had been implanted on patients in the United States and ninety-three thousand had been used worldwide. Despite having cleared FDA review as substantially equivalent to existing devices, the ASR was marketed by its manufacturer as a significant innovation and hence as worthy of a significantly higher price than those it replaced.

Warning signals soon dampened the initial enthusiasm for metal-on-metal hip implants. As early as 2007 the Australian joint replacement registry was reporting unusually high rates of failure and replacement for the ASR. It turned out that, despite their intuitive appeal, partial replacement surgery and metal-on-metal implant designs created greater risks for patients than did more traditional approaches and materials. The grinding of the metal thighbone on the metal pelvic socket shed microscopic particles that inflamed the surrounding tissue and, over time, caused tissue necrosis. Abrasion was increased by the angle of insertion in partial replacement procedures. The ASR experienced a failure rate of nearly 50 percent within six years after use, much higher than the rate for traditional models.[22]

The unfolding of the ASR story highlighted an unfortunate pattern of denial and cover-up. The manufacturer possessed evidence of excessive risk prior to market launch and continued to receive reports of adverse outcomes after launch. It had preliminary clinical studies and identified the risk of metal particles entering the surrounding tissue, but the FDA does not require manufacturers to submit results from internal studies or ·

to follow their preliminary studies with randomized clinical trials. The device was marketed heavily in Europe without clinical data. An internal report prepared by the manufacturer estimated that 36 percent of the implants would fail within five years, compared to the 5 percent industry average. So much money was at stake that the firm resisted calls for review, denied the validity of reported failure rates, and continued to insist the product was safe.[23] Eventually, however, the evidence became unmistakable. Much of the credit goes to device registries in Australia and England. In 2010 the manufacturer finally conducted a global recall of the product.

The fact that no new ASR hips were being used did not solve the dilemma facing the thousands of patients who already had received the implants. High rates of morbidity and revision surgery were being reported in every major nation. In 2011 the FDA required the manufacturer to conduct postmarket safety studies. The manufacturer delayed and by 2012 it still was not clear that surveillance was underway. The firm was rightfully worried about litigation. By the end of 2013 it faced more than ten thousand lawsuits from patients suffering adverse effects.[24] The manufacturer eventually offered a settlement exceeding $4 billion.[25]

It is important to draw the appropriate conclusions from the experience with metal-on-metal implants. The ASR was more than just an incremental modification of prostheses that had been in use for decades. It should have undergone PMA review because the novel material and design constituted a new product. The FDA could have and should have demanded small clinical trials to support the application for this incremental innovation even as part of the 510(k) clearance process. In 2011 the Institute of Medicine analyzed the 510(k) process and identified many disturbing flaws.[26] Unfortunately, the Institute recommended the full abandonment of the 510(k) pathway without offering any alternative. The Institute failed to recognize the implications of incremental innovation for the FDA regulatory process more generally and hence the necessity of the principle of substantial equivalence.

The ASR tragedy should not be used to justify overregulation of medical devices, nor to justify underregulation. It is appropriate for the FDA to rely heavily on PMA supplements, the 510(k) pathway, and substantial equivalence in the context of incremental innovation. However, it needs to ensure that regulatory flexibility does not undermine its mandate to ensure safety and effectiveness. Most immediately, the agency should require that all high-risk devices that were cleared as equivalent to products already on the market in 1976, and hence that never submitted clinical data, undergo PMA review. The FDA needs to require evidence of safety and effectiveness for intermediate-risk as well as high-risk products at periodic intervals, or when a device has undergone so many modifications that its clinical performance can no longer be inferred from that of previous models.

OVERREGULATION? TRANSCATHETER AORTIC VALVES

While some observers criticize the FDA for underregulation, permitting onto the market devices that are unsafe and ineffective, others criticize the agency for overregulation, preventing patient access to devices that offer significant benefits. These critics compare the FDA regulatory framework unfavorably to its European counterpart. The European Medicines Agency (EMA) regulates drugs in a manner broadly similar to the FDA, but does not wield comparable authority over implantable devices. Device regulation is the province of individual European nations, rather than the European Union, and is delegated by those nations to private organizations.[27] These independent "notified bodies" contract with device manufacturers to conduct reviews. The European framework does not require clinical evidence of effectiveness as a condition for market access.

The European regulatory approach has permitted rapid patient access to innovative devices that replace older and less effective treatments.[28] Easy access to the market can improve device performance, as manufacturers modify their designs, surgeons gain experience, and hospitals expand their clinical facilities. Early market access is particularly important for small device firms that lack the resources needed to complete a lengthy regulatory review. In part as a result of the differing regulatory frameworks, there are more small device firms in Europe than in the United States, and even large American firms often launch their products there before seeking access to the domestic market.

Nonsurgical valve replacement evolved from a diagnostic test in which a flexible plastic wire is inserted into the patient's femoral artery or another point of entry and then threaded through the vascular system. Light is powered along the catheter, allowing the cardiologist to study blockages, deformities, and other pathologies within the arteries and the heart without the need to cut them open. Diagnostic catheterization developed therapeutic applications when physicians attached a thin balloon onto the catheter and inflated it at points of vascular blockage. Balloon angioplasty was followed by catheter-based interventions that inserted stents to support continued function. Bare metal stents were succeeded by stents infused with anti-inflammatory drugs that inhibit the body's tendency to grow new tissue around the wire mesh and re-create the original blockage. Drug-eluting stents were launched in 2003 with simultaneous FDA authorization and Medicare coverage, an oft-cited but unfortunately rare example of regulatory efficiency.[29]

The technology of therapeutic catheterization evolved to the point where catheters could deliver compressed valves to replace those that had failed.[30] The compressed valve is positioned inside the aortic passageway and popped open, allowing blood through in one direction but preventing it from flowing back in the other.[31] The first two TAVR devices were approved in Europe in 2007. By 2011, when the first version gained FDA approval in the United States, transcatheter valves had already been approved for insurance coverage in 40 nations.[32]

The frontier of interventional cardiology subsequently moved from aortic to mitral valves, but FDA regulation continued to impede patient access and the evolution of the technology. Replacement of the mitral valve is a more complicated endeavor due to the fragile mitral anatomy and the lack of strong adjacent muscle tissue to which a new valve can be attached.[33] Surgical treatment of mitral valve disease emphasizes repair rather than replacement for these reasons. But although the engineering challenge for valve replacement is greater for the mitral than for the aortic valve, the potential benefit is also greater. Four million Americans have been diagnosed with moderate to severe mitral failure, compared to 1.2 million with aortic stenosis, and only 20 percent of patients with severe disease are eligible for surgery. Several mitral devices were approved and launched in Europe between 2008 and 2010 but, as of 2013, none had not been authorized for use in the United States.

Despite some clear advantages of the European regulatory framework for medical devices, accusations of FDA overregulation are misplaced. The European framework is fragmented across nations and independent review entities, which allows manufacturers to shop for the most lenient reviewer. The private review organizations face inherent conflicts of interests, since their ability to obtain contracts with manufacturers depends implicitly on the likelihood they will make a favorable evaluation. In contrast with the FDA regulatory process, where deliberations are conducted in public and decisions are published on the agency's website, data collected by the European review entities are considered business secrets. The delegated entities are not required to disclose the data they obtain nor the reasons they come to their evaluation.[34]

If the European device review process allows quick market access for beneficial devices, it also permits some unsafe products to obtain access. For example, a drug-eluting stent that received European market authorization in 2006 and was sold widely without clinical trials subsequently sought FDA authorization for use in the United States. The FDA required that it submit evidence of safety and effectiveness. When the required trials proved unsuccessful, the manufacturer abandoned its effort to gain access to the US market and subsequently removed the stent from the European market as well.[35] And it is worth repeating that the ASR metal-on-metal hip took advantage of the lenient European regulatory framework to launch there in 2003 prior to entering the US market.[36]

POSTMARKET SURVEILLANCE

Regulatory denial of market access is a blunt tool for protecting patients. It prevents access to treatments that appear unsafe or ineffective based on initial studies but that could improve their performance over time. And many treatments that are unacceptable for some applications can be used safely and effectively for others. The alternative is to facilitate initial market access while requiring ongoing surveillance and safe methods of use after launch. Postmarket surveillance permits patient access to promising technologies while doing a better job than premarket testing in identifying risks. The number of patients enrolled in premarket clinical trials is too small to detect subtle risks and benefits; the follow-up time is short for detecting long-term effects; and the patients enrolled in clinical trials are rarely representative of the broader population that eventually will use the therapy.

The FDA's traditional approach to postmarket surveillance relied on voluntary reports from manufacturers, hospitals, and physicians. These reports are inconsistent, incomplete, and lacking in information on the number of patients subjected to the treatment. More recently, the agency has sought to take advantage of data systems developed for other purposes. The agency has the capacity to query patient registries, medical records, and insurance claims, which significantly reduces the costs of postmarket surveillance. It has not sought to integrate the data systems itself, leaving data management and analysis to private organizations.[37] Postmarket surveillance and regulation are most fully developed for drugs that would pose unacceptable risks in some applications but offer benefits in others. At their best, the FDA's Risk Evaluation and Mitigation Strategies (REMS) allow clinical evidence to accumulate, patient targeting to improve, and refinements to be made in methods of drug administration.[38]

Formal postmarketing regulations are rare for implantable devices, but the agency has developed a few promising initiatives.

Market authorization for TAVR, for example, came with requirements both for surveillance and for limits on where the technology could be deployed. The agency was concerned that the procedure could be performed by physicians who lacked appropriate training and in hospitals that lacked advanced facilities. Practice makes perfect in cardiology, with the best outcomes and lowest costs achieved by high-volume practitioners.[39] And greater experience with one procedure often improves outcomes for other procedures. The FDA required hospitals seeking authorization to perform TAVR to have performed a high number of related surgical and angioplasty procedures and to have in place a multidisciplinary team of cardiologists, cardiac surgeons, imaging specialists, anesthesiologists, intensive care specialists, and rehabilitation experts.

The FDA was also concerned that patients would be subjected to TAVR when they ought to be treated surgically or, on the contrary, that they would be subjected to surgery when the less invasive TAVR procedure would be appropriate. There had been considerable competition between cardiologists and cardiac surgeons over the use of drug-eluting stents, which significantly reduced patient demand for open-heart surgery. To avoid similar competition over valve replacement, the FDA embraced the principle of "rational dispersion."[40] The various cardiac professional societies developed criteria to triage patients between catheter-based valve replacement, surgical valve replacement, and medical treatment without valve replacement. The guidelines also covered operative processes, postsurgical recovery, and postdischarge care. Process and outcome data were to be compiled in data registries, including the device used, the surgeon, the hospital, the patient's self-assessed quality of life, and clinical indicators thirty days after surgery. The TAVR registry accommodates modifications in the device, includes off-label along with on-label uses, and records patient outcomes over time. It is coordinated with existing registries that capture data on 80 percent of patients undergoing cardiac catheterization and 95 percent of patients undergoing cardiac surgery.

NECESSARY BUT NOT SUFFICIENT

The FDA's mission is to prevent the use of medical technologies whose risks outweigh their benefits. It is impossible to imagine a modern health care system that allows toxic or ineffective treatments to be administered to patients who lack the ability to evaluate scientific evidence. But it is also important for the FDA to minimize the costs of complying with its regulations so as not to unduly limit patient access and impede innovation.

The FDA's traditional regulatory model does not match the reality of much medical innovation. The safety and effectiveness of a drug or device cannot be fully assessed under research conditions prior to launch, but must be studied over the entire life cycle of its use in the real world. Many medical technologies improve over time, based on experience and experimentation with better models, materials, and methods of use. Even technologies whose physical structure is fixed, such as drug molecules, can become more safe and effective as they are targeted more precisely, are combined with other products based on well-developed clinical protocols, and are embedded in treatment regimes that encourage patient adherence and engagement. The process of regulation should not be a one-time event but, rather, should be a continuous process that combines early and easy access to the market with rigorous postlaunch surveillance and control.

It is not realistic to expect the FDA to singlehandedly assure safe and effective uses of medical technologies. Other entities should play important roles. Insurers can promote appropriate use through coverage policy, medical management, and network contracting. Hospitals can manage their drug and device supply chains in an efficient manner. Physicians can modify treatments if the risks prove larger and the benefits smaller than anticipated. Patients can weigh risks and benefits in light of their own values and preferences. FDA regulation of market access is necessary but not sufficient for ensuring the appropriate use of medical technology.

2

Insurance Coverage and Reimbursement

Patients may use any FDA-approved therapy prescribed by any physician, if they are willing to pay with their own money. As a practical matter, however, most new tests and treatments will be used only if their costs are covered by health insurance. Insurance expands access to valuable medical technologies, thereby promoting health and reducing disability, but it also accelerates the growth in spending. Insured patients use more services, and shop less carefully, than do patients who pay with their own money. Insurers pass the costs from this greater medical use and price on to the governmental programs, private employers, and individual subscribers who pay insurance premiums. These payers see their insurance premiums rising more rapidly than their incomes, year after year, and fret that health care is squeezing out other worthy goals. They now look to insurers not merely to finance their health care, but to make it cheaper.

Insurers wield several instruments in pursuit of their dual mission to expand access and restrain costs. The potentially most important is coverage policy, which specifies the treatments that will be reimbursed and which, by exclusion, must be paid directly by the patient. This decision to extend or restrict coverage is a blunt instrument for promoting appropriate use, however, since most treatments are effective in some contexts but ineffective in others. Insurers thus supplement coverage policy by medical management, which limits reimbursement for each technology to particular indications and settings. Insurers also contract selectively with hospitals, channeling higher volumes of patients to facilities willing to document their quality and discount their prices.

This chapter analyzes the role of insurance as the second stage, after FDA regulation of market access, in the purchasing of medical technology. It begins with Medicare as the nation's bellwether insurer. Medicare has the scale and sophistication to make evidence-based coverage decisions and to deny coverage to technologies where the financial costs exceed the health benefits. But Medicare is under pressure from manufacturers and patients who want their favored products to be covered, regardless of cost and comparative effectiveness. The agency must tread carefully. The chapter then shifts focus to private insurers, and analyzes medical management programs that limit costly technologies to appropriate conditions and settings. It concludes with insurers' strategies for promoting Centers of Excellence for high-value medical technologies.

COVERAGE POLICY

When Medicare was created in 1965, its authors specified that the program would cover tests and treatments provided in a hospital, physician's office, or other accredited facility if the services were "reasonable and necessary."[1] This vague term might seem to cover any service recommended by any physician. In practice, it has come to mean that Medicare cannot exclude coverage simply because a new product is less effective or more expensive than already-covered treatments. Medical technologies typically needed to obtain FDA approval. But then Medicare usually would reimburse any use of the product, even when prescribed for indications or in settings different from those authorized by the FDA. Private health plans followed Medicare's lead in adopting inclusive coverage criteria.

Over time, Medicare and private insurers have developed more sophisticated standards for deciding which products and procedures will be eligible for reimbursement. But coverage decision-making is plagued with contentious scientific, ethical, and political debates. How will coverage be decided for products with incomplete evidence of risks and benefits? What is the relevance of comparative effectiveness, the performance of a new product relative to existing alternatives? What is the appropriate role for costs and cost effectiveness?

National Coverage Decision-Making

The Centers for Medicare and Medicaid Services (CMS) initiates formal Medicare coverage reviews for technologies and procedures that are likely to improve quality, increase costs, or impose adverse side effects. The centerpiece is the process of national coverage determination, which establishes uniform policies for the nation.[2] In principle, national coverage reviews are based on high-quality evidence from laboratory tests, clinical trials, and real-world experience, developed in consultation with experts in medicine, engineering, patient advocacy, economics, and medical ethics. In practice, the process falls short of its ideal.

In its fifty years of existence, CMS has issued only three hundred national coverage decisions, despite the thousands of new products and procedures that have come into regular use.[3] The agency sometimes seems to be running behind the dynamic of innovation. Many products receive coverage through decisions made by private entities that administer claims payment for the agency, despite their lack of scientific expertise. Even more new products are covered implicitly, without any formal review, if they are used by hospitals that are paid by Medicare on a case rate basis.

Medicare's selection of products for national coverage does not reflect a coherent policy framework.[4] For example, in 2008 the agency issued a list of twenty widely used technologies for which the evidence of effectiveness was unclear, as a priority list for national coverage reviews. But the agency lacked the staff to implement its priorities and was hampered by continual leadership turnover. The priority list was never updated or expanded, and only a few of the technologies ever were reviewed. There have been no further efforts at developing coverage priorities. The quality of the assessments made as part of national coverage decisions has also been subject to criticism.[5] Complete evidence on risks and benefits is typically lacking at the time of review, but the agency is under pressure from patients and providers to extend coverage. The outcome of a national coverage review is almost always a positive decision.[6]

National coverage reviews have become quite complex, with an increasing number of limitations being placed on new technologies that do obtain Medicare coverage. The first coverage decision that contained limitations was for organ transplantation. Reimbursement was authorized only for specified clinical conditions, for physicians with special expertise, and for hospitals meeting volume criteria. In the 1990s CMS issued coverage decisions with limitations for a wider set of technologies, including ventricular assist devices, bariatric surgery, implantable defibrillators, and carotid stents. Coverage with limitations subsequently has become the norm. CMS now restricts coverage to patients with severe disease (56 percent of national coverage decisions), who have failed first-line therapy (19 percent), or who are enrolled in clinical trials (19 percent). It limits coverage to uses within a specified treatment regimen (17 percent), within a specified clinical setting (16 percent), or when they are accompanied by a specified diagnostic test (25 percent).[7]

Limitations offer the means for the agency to extend coverage to new technologies that are beneficial when used appropriately but that often are used outside the boundaries of the evidence. But the limitations have no effective enforcement mechanism. In this, CMS coverage restrictions are analogous to FDA restrictions on drug or device marketing outside the approved product label. Studies have found no changes in patterns of use for a new medical technology after CMS imposes limits on coverage.[8]

Most coverage decisions are not made centrally by CMS but are delegated to private organizations that operate in fifteen geographic regions. The quality of these local coverage decisions falls far short of the already-inadequate national decisions. The local organizations' primary function is to pay insurance claims, not to conduct scientific reviews. Their decisions are sometimes based on high-quality clinical trials, but often merely cite observational reports. Some decisions cite no evidence at all.[9] Local coverage decisions apply only to the states where the organizations have jurisdiction, creating regional differences and disparities.[10] This geographic variability has declined over time, however, as local CMS contractors have merged into larger regional organizations.[11]

Coverage with Evidence Development

Evidence on the safety and effectiveness of a new medical technology is often incomplete at the time the coverage decision needs to be made. Yet there is great pressure from patients and manufacturers to extend coverage quickly, even if the needed data will only emerge through follow-on clinical trials or observational studies.

This dilemma could be dealt with by making insurance coverage conditional on the continued gathering of data. Coverage with Evidence Development (CED) was pioneered by the Medicare program when faced with requests to extend coverage of implantable defibrillators from severely ill patients, where there existed good evidence of benefit, to less ill patients, for whom comparable evidence was lacking.[12] Under the CED policy, Medicare agrees to reimburse a treatment only if patients are enrolled in a clinical trial or some other mechanism for systematic data gathering. The new data are to be included in a registry that, over time, can yield scientifically valid evidence on patterns of benefit and harm. Medicare can specify the design of the follow-up studies to ensure they are relevant to the eventual coverage decision, such as requiring sufficient numbers of patients with a particular clinical indication. Coverage decisions are conditional in the sense that they are valid only until a subsequent review can be conducted. In principle, coverage can be rescinded if the follow-up analyses do not support the original performance expectations.

Medicare has applied CED to more than a dozen national coverage decisions. Unfortunately, the needed data have often not been collected in a manner that sheds light on the question of whether coverage should be sustained. For example, data for the high-profile defibrillator registry did not begin to include information on the firing of the device in response to changes in patient symptoms, the key characteristic of concern to Medicare, until five years after the initiation of the registry. In other cases, the appropriate follow-on studies were never conducted at all, and coverage continued despite the inadequate evidence of benefit. In some cases physicians and hospitals have been slow or unwilling to provide data to the registries. Follow-on studies have been used as part of coverage decision-making for only two technologies. In both cases, the decisions were more permissive than could be justified by the new evidence.[13] Politics trumped science.

Coverage with Evidence Development is an appealing principle. Not only should coverage decisions evolve in step with the clinical evidence, the coverage process itself can serve as a lever to improve the evidence. However, sustained opposition and a lack of clear statutory authority have limited the implementation of CED. The pharmaceutical and medical device industries have opposed conditional coverage, which they often interpret as a method for raising the regulatory bar even higher. Private insurers have embraced conditional coverage in principle but have not implemented it in practice, due to reluctance to fund follow-up studies and out of concern for the administrative costs of repeated reviews.[14] CMS may conclude that the administrative and political costs of the strategy outweigh its benefits.

The Role of Comparative Effectiveness

Coverage policy should systematically incorporate evidence on the comparative performance of each new treatment. In every other part of the economy, the question "does this thing work?"

is followed immediately by "how well does it work compared to what we already have?" Assessment of comparative performance is important since many new products are similar to existing treatments and offer few new benefits. For example, of the 645 drugs approved by the FDA between 1987 and 2011, only 32 percent created a genuinely new form of treatment.[15] Another 22 percent offered minor improvements in performance and 46 percent simply replicated the effects of existing products.

There is a striking paucity of evidence comparing the performance of new technologies with alternatives.[16] The FDA does not require comparisons with existing treatments as a condition for market access. Manufacturers lack the incentive to conduct comparative analyses, since they run the risk that their product would not prove superior to its competitors. Insurers would benefit from comparative effectiveness research but each health plan shirks the funding of needed studies.

In recent years the federal government has increased its financial support for comparative effectiveness research. In 2010 it established the Patient Centered Outcomes Research Institute (PCORI) to establish research priorities and disseminate findings.[17] The legislation focused on improving decision-making by individual physicians and patients, not on coverage decision-making. Indeed, Medicare has faced strong opposition from manufacturers to the use of comparative effectiveness in coverage policy, and the 2010 legislation imposes several explicit limitations.[18] CMS cannot base a coverage decision solely on comparative effectiveness, though it can incorporate comparative assessments along with other evidence of medical necessity. Comparative effectiveness research cannot be used to limit coverage for treatments that affect terminally ill patients or for those with disabilities. As a practical matter, CMS has never used comparative effectiveness in these discriminatory ways. But political opposition has blunted Medicare's interest in comparative performance as a coverage criterion. Private insurers have followed Medicare's lead, and are cautious in denying coverage to new treatments even if existing products are equally effective.

The Role of Cost Effectiveness

It makes no sense for an insurer to reimburse a technology that offers benefits similar to those of existing treatments while charging a higher price. Neither the taxpayer nor the employer is willing to fund everything that the life sciences industry can create. The statutory and political context is quite hostile, however, to the inclusion of cost as a coverage criterion. Medicare's "reasonable and necessary" principle would seem to require reimbursement of any treatment that offers any incremental benefit, no matter how small, regardless of the incremental cost, no matter how large. For their part, private insurers are unwilling to be seen as rationing access to care on the basis of costs.

There are two contexts in which cost could be used in coverage policy. Some new products generate outcomes equivalent to, but not better than, existing treatments. Here the insurer could use the principle of "least costly alternative," declaring itself unwilling to pay more than the lowest price charged by any equally effective alternative. Medicare has used the principle of least costly alternative in some contexts, especially for durable medical equipment.[19] Private insurers often restrict drug coverage to a subset of products within each therapeutic class. They exclude some providers from their networks to obtain favorable rates from the others. Insurers in some European nations limit drug reimbursement to the price of the least costly therapeutic equivalent.

The principle of least costly alternative could and should be used as part of CMS reimbursement policy.[20] Medicare frequently finds itself obligated to extend coverage to follow-on technologies that charge substantially more than existing treatments without offering incremental benefits. Medicare could pay the manufacturer's list price only for a defined period, such as three years, during which time evidence would be gathered on the new treatment. If the new evidence proved clinical superiority, Medicare could continue to reimburse the new product at its list price. However, if the evidence indicated that the new product was not superior to an existing alternative, the price could be reduced to that of the reference product.

The criterion of least costly alternative only applies to products that have direct substitutes, but many technologies have none. Economists have developed cost effectiveness analysis (CEA) to help decision-makers establish priorities among products that offer different mixes of costs and benefits.[21] CEA divides the benefit of a technology by its price to obtain the cost per unit of benefit, such as "quality-adjusted life year." Ratios can be compared across treatments. A technology that extends life by five years is valued five times more than a competitor that extends life by only one year. A treatment that extends life by a year of full health and functional ability is valued more highly than a treatment that offers a year plagued by discomfort and disability.

Cost effectiveness rankings do not settle the insurer's question as to which technologies should be covered by insurance. The rankings can be used, however, if the insurer establishes a threshold to what it will pay per quality-adjusted life year, extending coverage to all treatments whose cost ratio falls below the threshold and denying coverage to others. Some other nations have established explicit thresholds,[22] which they use as part of price negotiations with technology firms. A manufacturer that wants its product to be covered needs to reduce its price below the threshold. Without a threshold, either implicit or explicit, there is no limit to what manufacturers could charge. Nations that rely on cost effectiveness make exceptions to their coverage thresholds for particularly important technologies, such as cancer drugs.[23]

Cost effectiveness has rarely been used either by Medicare or by private insurers in the United States. CMS does use cost effectiveness in establishing coverage for preventive as distinct from therapeutic services. More importantly, the agency seems to consider cost implicitly in its decisions. Technologies whose applications for national coverage include a favorable cost effectiveness analysis are more likely to obtain their goal than technologies lacking supportive cost effectiveness data.[24] Nevertheless, cost effectiveness analysis has served as a lightening rod for popular fears over the rationing of care. Some critics highlight methodological limitations. Others argue that the quality-adjusted life year index discriminates against treatments for very sick patients.[25] Congress has explicitly banned cost effectiveness analysis from Medicare coverage policy.[26] Private insurers have avoided explicit reference to costs, and argue that their coverage decisions are based solely on clinical benefits and risks.

MEDICAL MANAGEMENT

Many technologies are safe and effective for some conditions, but hazardous and ineffective for others. Coverage policy focuses on whether a test or treatment improves outcomes for any patient, not on the benefits for a particular individual. Insurers thus supplement coverage policy with medical management. They assess appropriateness by comparing the reimbursement claims they receive for a patient's test or treatment with evidence-based clinical protocols. These protocols are developed by academic medical centers, professional societies, and governmental research organizations, building on published studies and filling in gaps using professional opinion. Medical management is the responsibility of the insurer's physicians and nurses, with difficult cases referred to the Chief Medical Officer. Reimbursement is approved if the proposed use is in accord with the protocol or can be justified by special characteristics of the patient.[27]

The criteria specified by medical management vary across different technologies. Some treatments impose risks that are only justified for patients with severe illness, such as toxic chemotherapies for cancer patients, while others should only be used on comparatively healthy patients able to withstand the treatment's toxicity. Some criteria focus on patient engagement, authorizing reimbursement only for patients enrolled in weight loss, smoking cessation, or nurse-led home care programs. Targeted drugs known to be effective only on patients with particular genetic markers are reimbursed when the patient has tested positive on the relevant diagnostic test. Particularly expensive treatments may be covered only if the patient has already tried less costly alternatives.

The theoretical case for medical management is strong, since technologies impose avoidable cost and harm if used inappropriately. In the real world, however, medical management programs have fallen far short of their potential. Indeed, most do not merit the term "medical management" and should be referred to as utilization management, since they focus on costs without adequate attention to clinical need. Utilization management programs create administrative burdens for physicians and confusing requirements for patients. Physicians understandably resent second-guessing by insurers. Patients resent interference with their choices, and find sympathetic ears in the court of public opinion. Popular hostility was responsible for much of the backlash against managed care in the 1990s, and some insurers experimented with a full abandonment of utilization management. Unfortunately, those that abandoned medical management found they were reimbursing numerous examples of unnecessary care. Most health plans thus have retained medical management, but limit it to often-misused treatments.[28]

CONTRACTING FOR LOWER PRICES

There are large and unjustified differences in the prices charged for the same tests and treatments. The prices charged by hospitals for cardiac surgery, by clinics for diagnostic radiology, and by laboratories for blood tests can range more than fivefold, even within the same local market. In part this reflects the market power of particular providers. Some hospitals have consolidated into chains that account for a very high percentage of the total capacity in the market. They can brush off insurers' demands for price discounts. The price variation also reflects the clinical setting where a technology is used. A surgical procedure will usually be priced higher if performed in an ambulatory surgery center than in a physician's office, and higher yet if performed in a hospital-based outpatient department. An infused drug is usually priced lower if obtained through a specialty distributor and administered in an physician's office than if administered through a hospital-based infusion center.

Examples of the range of prices charged for orthopedic and cardiac procedures can be seen in figure 2, reflecting the experience of over thirty thousand patients in sixty-one hospitals across eight states.[29] The average Medicare payment is presented as a standard of comparison. Medicare establishes a reimbursement level based on a national administrative formula that is not vulnerable to price demands from consolidated hospital systems.

As illustrated in figure 2, in 2008 Medicare paid an average of $13,000 for knee and hip replacement surgery; $16,000 for cervical spine fusion, cardiac pacemaker insertion, and coronary angioplasty; $26,000 for lumbar spine fusion; and $37,000 for insertion of an cardiac defibrillator.[30] The prices charged to private insurers were substantially higher. Especially striking are the differences between prices charged in competitive and concentrated markets. Prices for knee and hip replacement averaged $19,000 in competitive markets, for example, but $28,000 in concentrated markets, a difference of 47 percent. Prices in concentrated markets were 30 percent higher than in competitive markets for spine and cardiac procedures. Hospitals in concentrated markets charged an average of $36,000 for implanting a drug-eluting stent, $32,000 for implanting a pacemaker, and $64,000 for implanting a defibrillator. In competitive markets, procedure prices averaged $20,000 for stents, $22,000 for pacemakers, and $47,000 for defibrillators.

The contribution margins earned by hospitals for these technologically sophisticated procedures are measured as the difference between the revenues received and the direct costs incurred.[31] Margins ranged from 44 percent on defibrillator

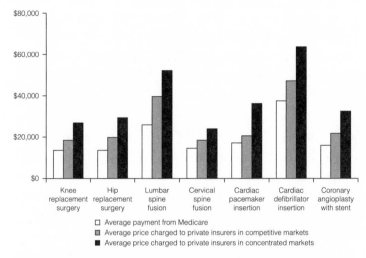

Figure 2. Market power and pricing: prices paid by Medicare and by private insurers in competitive and consolidated markets for major surgical procedures.

insertion to 62 percent on knee replacement and coronary angioplasty. The percentage profit margins were similar between concentrated and competitive markets, but the dollar margins were much higher.

CONTRACTING FOR PRICE AND QUALITY

For some highly specialized procedures and technologies, insurers seek to channel patients to a limited number of hospitals. Some of these Centers of Excellence programs focus on a single procedure, such as coronary artery bypass, while others cover an entire service line, such as interventional cardiology. Hospitals that seek designation as a Center of Excellence must document good clinical outcomes and then negotiate a case rate that covers all the drugs, devices, and diagnostic tests used during the admission. Most of the case rates also cover the services provided by attending physicians.

Insurers that contract with Centers of Excellence expand the geographic scope of health care markets by inducing enrollees to travel further for their care. This brings more providers potentially into competition with one another. Competition among hospitals is usually limited by the fact that many markets are small, while other markets have consolidated through mergers and acquisitions.[32] Patient travel expands the scope of the competitive market from the city to the region.[33] This regionalization works best for procedures that can be scheduled in advance, such as organ transplantation, spine fusion, open-heart surgery, and treatment of complex cancers. Many of these involve high-cost and high-performance medical technologies.

Lowes, a national chain of home improvement stores with two hundred thousand employees and retirees, has pursued a Center of Excellence strategy for cardiac procedures.[34] Lowes had been concerned about the wide variation in hospital prices, complications, and readmissions, and in April 2010 launched a program for cardiac angioplasty, bypass surgery, and valve replacement. After an analysis of competing hospitals, Lowes developed a national relationship with the Cleveland Clinic in Ohio. The Clinic had a strong reputation for quality and was willing to offer attractive prices to obtain patients from outside its geographic area. Lowes structured the Center of Excellence as a supplemental benefit for its employees, not as a requirement. Employees that selected cardiac care outside the Cleveland Clinic remained responsible for their usual cost sharing. If they chose the Clinic, however, the cost sharing was waived. The patients were also reimbursed for travel costs. Lowes experienced meaningful cost reductions from its relationship and expanded it to surgical and nonsurgical treatment for back pain. In collaboration with WalMart and the Pacific Business Group on Health, Lowes then expanded its Centers of Excellence program to orthopedic joint replacement.[35]

Competition can be strengthened if the market is expanded even further to encompass facilities in Europe and Asia that perform at US levels of quality. In 2013 the *New York Times* examined international medical travel for orthopedic surgery and described the choices made by a number of American patients.[36] One article featured an architect and snowboard enthusiast who was forced to stop work and abandon leisure activities due to debilitating arthritis. His insurance refused to cover hip replacement, since his arthritis stemmed from an earlier sports injury and was deemed a preexisting condition. He sought to negotiate an affordable rate with his local hospital, but was told he would face a charge of $13,000 for the artificial hip implant, another $65,000 for the hospital stay, additional fees from the surgeon and anesthesiologist, and charges for postoperative physical therapy. If he suffered a complication requiring revision or readmission, the charges would be doubled. He chose to receive his hip replacement at a hospital in Belgium, which charged him at total of $13,600.

THE LIMITS OF INSURERS AS PURCHASERS

There is a strong cultural skepticism in the United States concerning the role of insurers in managing the cost of care. Many other nations trust public insurance programs to assess the effectiveness and establish reimbursement levels for new medical technologies. Less trust is found in the United States, in part due to the private and for-profit ownership of many health plans.

But the distrust also extends to nonprofit insurers and to governmental programs. Even modest efforts to set priorities for reimbursement are often vilified as intrusions into personal decisions. The skepticism is embodied in the legislative and judicial limits on coverage with evidence development, comparative effectiveness research, and cost effectiveness analysis. For private insurers, almost any limitation on reimbursement is an invitation for litigation.

Insurance coverage policy, medical management, and network contracting will play continuing but only modest roles in promoting the appropriate use of medical technology. Their instruments are too blunt and popular skepticism is too strong. Most of the work will be done elsewhere. Value-based purchasing is shifting to physicians, hospitals, and patients themselves.

3

Methods of Payment for
Medical Technology

The US health care system has historically paid separately for each test, treatment, procedure, and patient visit to a physician or hospital. Payment for knee replacement surgery has typically included one fee for the surgeon, another for the anesthesiologist, and another for the attending internist. A per-case or per-day fee is paid to the hospital for its staffing and facilities and a supplemental fee covers the implanted artificial knee. Additional fees are paid for exceptionally long hospital stays, readmissions to the hospital, use of a nursing home, and physical therapy offered in an ambulatory clinic.

Fee-for-service reimbursement encourages the adoption of new technologies, providing the revenues to fund research and development. But it creates no incentives for technologies to be used on the patients most likely to benefit, in the most appropriate settings, and according to evidence-based clinical guidelines. Each clinical participant is paid independently, and so none has the incentive to be concerned with the quality and cost of the services provided by others. Most importantly for the medical technology sector, fee-for-service payment often reimburses the technology itself separately from the procedures that administer it. Physician offices, hospitals, ambulatory surgery centers, and other facilities purchase drugs, devices, or imaging equipment from the manufacturers and then bill the insurer for their use. They often increase the price by a percentage markup. For example, some implanted devices purchased by hospitals are subject to a 250 percent markup when reimbursement is demanded from insurers. This creates the incentive to use the most expensive brands and models, since markups are typically established as a percentage above the acquisition price.

Every new intervention brings a new payment, and often an additional profit opportunity. No wonder health care costs are so high and patient outcomes so variable. The system delivers what it is rewarded for delivering: more care, but not always better care.

Health insurers are now experimenting with new methods for paying physicians and hospitals, including case rates, episode payments, and population-based payments. Reimbursement for drugs, devices, and diagnostics will increasingly be bundled into a single payment for the patient's entire course of care, rather than be reimbursed individually. In this context, innovations that reduce costs will be embraced. The new payment methods will motivate physicians to prescribe generic over branded drugs, perform procedures in ambulatory rather than inpatient facilities, and closely monitor patients after hospital discharge. They will favor hospitals that are judicious in their assessment and procurement of imaging equipment and implantable devices.

But caution is in order. If not designed intelligently, the new methods of payment will reduce the use of high-cost new technologies, even if those technologies also improve outcomes. What happens when a manufacturer develops an imaging modality that improves the precision of surgery, but requires a major capital investment? What happens when surgery can be replaced by less invasive catheter-based interventions, reducing hospital complications and length of stay, but at the price of an expensive implantable device? How will treatment choices be affected? How can payment be structured so as not to penalize innovation?

This chapter analyzes the emerging forms of physician and hospital payment to assess their impact on the purchasing and use of medical technology. It describes fee for service and then examines case rates, episode payments, and population-based payments as means to motivate efficient selection and provision of technology. It then considers mechanisms for adjusting the payment methods to ensure that providers are adequately reimbursed for the adoption of expensive but quality-improving new treatments.

FEE FOR SERVICE

Fee-for-service payment is the natural form of reimbursement for health care services provided in a fragmented manner by caregivers who do not share a common organization or culture. Each participant in the patient's course of care is paid for the particular contribution made, without regard to the quantity or quality of the contributions made by others, and without regard to whether the final outcome for the patient was the best that could be obtained. The underlying ethos is one of independence and autonomy. You don't monitor and seek to manage the services I provide, and I won't monitor and manage yours.

The foundation of the traditional payment system is the fee schedule for professional services, which specifies a price to be paid for each of the thousands of different interventions that physicians can perform for their patients. Some coherence is created by "relative value scales" that assign weights to each particular intervention, thereby allowing insurers to assign prices by simply multiplying the weights by a dollar conversion factor. Medicare's "Resource-Based Relative Value Scale" performs this function for the innumerable professional codes, and has been adopted by many private insurers even if they apply different, and typically more generous, dollar conversion factors.

Some supplies and equipment are implicitly bundled into fee-for-service payment rates. For example, a physician would not be paid an additional fee to cover the cost of bandages applied to a simple wound or for the use of a stethoscope to diagnose a respiratory infection. But clinically and economically important supplies and equipment do bring additional reimbursement. Oncologists and rheumatologists who infuse biopharmaceuticals into patients suffering from cancer, rheumatoid arthritis, and other serious conditions submit to the insurer one claim to cover the drug and a separate to cover the infusion process. The drug claim is the more important, since the physicians historically have been permitted to charge the insurer at a rate much higher than the one paid by the physician to the drug manufacturer. Similarly, physicians who order expensive imaging tests to patients submit one claim for the test itself, often referred to as the technical or facility fee, and a second one for the act of interpreting the result. The technical fee is the most important one, since it usually exceeds greatly the actual cost of supplying one more test. The same logic applies to expensive implantable devices. Hospitals and ambulatory surgery centers submit one claim to the insurer to cover the surgical procedure itself and another to cover the artificial joint, valve, or pacemaker used as part of the procedure. And yes, the provider's profit margin on the device typically is much higher than the margin on the surgery.

Fee for service has offered some important benefits to the health care system. Volume-based reimbursement encourages physicians to adopt new tests and treatments as soon as they become available, accelerating access for patients in need of care. It encourages hospitals to build state-of-the-art clinical facilities to support and showcase the new technological opportunities. Separate reimbursement for drugs, devices, and diagnostic tests allows physicians to prescribe and administer them without using resources that could be devoted to other purposes. More generally, fee for service has rewarded the adoption of new medical technologies, spurred investments in research and development, and fueled the engine of innovation. The US health care system has featured both fee-for-service technology reimbursement, for which it is regularly criticized, and the world's most innovative technology industry, for which it is regularly praised.

This structure of payment is also seriously dysfunctional. It is hard to imagine how automobiles would perform if the consumer paid one fee to the manufacturer for the chassis and additional separate fees to each independent supplier for the transmission and the brakes. It is one thing for airlines to charge passengers extra fees for the meals supplied in the air, but what if each pilot and copilot submitted a supplemental charge to each passenger? Given fee-for-service payment incentives, it is not surprising that entrepreneurial physicians develop infusion centers, acquire diagnostic radiology equipment, and invest in ambulatory surgery centers. It is not surprising that entrepreneurial hospitals employ physicians and create infusion capabilities, radiology clinics, and surgery centers within their own walls. And it certainly is not surprising that pharmaceutical, device, and medical equipment firms employ large sales staffs to ensure that their products are embraced and used with enthusiasm.

CASE RATE PAYMENT

A fundamental flaw in the purchasing of health care is the mismatch between the unit of care and the unit of payment. Drugs, devices, imaging tests, and surgical procedures are components of larger episodes of care. But fee-for-service payment reimburses them as if the selection, placement, and timing of each component within the larger episode were not important. Perhaps some simple forms of care can be reimbursed effectively by fee for service. But most services, and certainly those responsible for the most spending, require coordination with other components of care. They are best reimbursed as part of a payment that covers an entire care episode.

Important progress has been made over the past two decades. Medicare reimburses hospitals with a single fee for all the services used within an admission, adjusted for the principal diagnoses and procedures performed. The payment for knee replacement surgery, for example, covers the costs of operating room staff, the implanted prosthesis, medications used during and after the procedure, and the physical therapy delivered prior to discharge. CMS establishes a single rate for each Diagnosis Related Group (DRG) and updates the rates to account for changes in costs and clinical standards that are outside the control of the hospital.[1] The DRG rate does not include the services of the physicians, however, or the services provided before or after the hospital stay. Private insurers often don't bundle the components of a hospital stay, paying separately for the implantable device and for each day the patient remains in the facility.

Case rates give hospitals incentives to pay attention to the cost of their services, and the implementation of Medicare's DRG system exerted a powerful effect on hospital behavior. Under fee for service, each extra test, treatment, and day in the facility generated extra revenue. There was no reward for cost control, for saying no to higher wages, for negotiating lower prices with suppliers, or for extending the life of capital equipment. On the contrary, reductions in costs brought reductions in revenues. Under case rates, by way of contrast, additional expenditures hurt rather than help the hospital's bottom line. Increased expenditures on medical technology cannot simply be passed on to the insurer for reimbursement.[2]

After it was introduced, the DRG system led to a significant slowdown in hospital cost growth, due primarily to better discharge planning and shorter lengths of patient stay.[3] Patient recovery shifted from the hospital to rehabilitation facilities, nursing homes, and home health care. Over time, case rates encouraged many form of surgery to move from costly inpatient to more efficient outpatient settings. These changes did not impair quality and, indeed, the outcomes experienced by Medicare patients continued to improve throughout the years of DRG implementation.[4]

Private insurers have lagged behind Medicare in shifting toward case rate payment. They usually negotiate a daily rate or a percentage discount off the hospitals' list prices, which retains the hospital's incentive to do more to earn more. Many insurers carve medical devices out of the base payment and reimburse them separately. The carve-outs persist indefinitely, even after the devices no longer can be considered innovative. Many insurers are forced to reimburse more for medical devices than the rates actually paid by hospitals to the manufacturers, giving hospitals an additional incentive to use expensive inputs. Some medical device firms advise hospitals on how to carve out and bill additionally for implantable devices in order to reduce resistance to device price increases.[5]

The potential savings from a shift to case rate payment can be seen in table 1, which presents the distribution of prices paid in 2008 for patients using any of six major categories of joint, spine, and cardiac devices.[6]

Why would hospitals pay such different rates for similar inputs? Detailed analyses of knee and hip devices found that only 3 percent of the price variance was due to the patient's age, disease severity, or comorbidities.[7] Approximately half of the variance was due to differences in the prices negotiated with manufacturers, reflecting the hospitals' scale and physician alignment. The remaining variance was due to choices by different surgeons operating in the same hospitals, even after adjusting for patient characteristics.

The potential benefit from shifting to case rates can also be seen in the patients' length of stay. Length of stay depends on the effectiveness of postsurgical care and discharge planning. For the patients represented in table 1, the average hospital stay ranged from 2.4 to 6.0 days for knee replacement, from 1.0 to 4.4 days for cervical spine fusion, and from 1.0 to 9.9 days for pacemaker insertion. Similar variability was observed for the other procedures.

The length of stay in the hospital also depends on whether the patient suffered a surgical complication. For the patients

TABLE 1

Variance across hospitals in prices paid for implantable devices

	Artificial Knee Implants	Artificial Hip Implants	Lumbar Spine Implants	Cervical Spine Implants	Cardiac Pacemakers	Cardiac Defibrillators
Minimum	$3,380	$3,828	$3,397	$2,008	$4,925	$19,150
25th percentile	$4,463	$5,425	$5,425	$3,056	$5,709	$22,870
Median	$4,925	$6,238	$6,238	$4,106	$6,197	$25,066
75th percentile	$6,549	$7,262	$7,262	$5,881	$7,024	$28,599
Maximum	$10,944	$10,640	$29,311	$10,133	$10,790	$34,961

represented in table 1, the percentage suffering a serious complication ranged across hospitals from 0 percent to 24 percent for hip replacement, from 0 percent to 76 percent for lumbar spine fusion, and from 0 percent to 33 percent for insertion of a defibrillator. Similar variance was observed for the other procedures. These differences in length of stay reflect different rates of complications during the hospital stay. Complications that happen after patient discharge add further to the cost and morbidity, but are not included in these measures.

Rates of readmission are very high for Medicare patients. A 2003 study reported readmission rates of 20 percent within one month of discharge, 45 percent within six months, and 55 percent within one year. The highest rates were for medical causes such as pneumonia, but surgical cases also experienced rates of 16 percent at one month and 47 percent at one year.[8] One-month readmission rates were 15 percent for cardiac stent placement, with the major cause being failure of the stent procedure itself, and 10 percent for hip and knee replacement, with the major cause being postoperative complications. Readmission rates for younger and healthier enrollees in private health insurance are lower. Approximately 1 percent of patients undergoing knee replacement surgery in five major hospital systems suffered a major complication prior to discharge and 2.4 percent were readmitted to the hospital within thirty days after discharge.[9]

EPISODE PAYMENT

Medicare's case rates do not cover the hospitalized patient's entire course of care. Laboratory and radiological tests provided prior to admission are reimbursed separately on a fee-for-service basis, even if they are done in preparation for surgery.

Postdischarge care, including follow-up visits, occupational therapy, outpatient and inpatient rehabilitation, and recovery in a nursing home, is also reimbursed on a supplemental basis. If the patient experiences a complication and is readmitted to the hospital, Medicare makes an additional payment rather than expecting the hospital to warranty its services.

The truncation of case rates limits the rewards for care coordination. Indeed, narrow case rates create incentives for services to be moved out of the hospital for additional reimbursement rather than coordinated as part of the admission. Medicare's DRG system led to an expansion in ambulatory diagnostic and surgery centers, postacute facilities, home health agencies, and other entities that escaped the bounds of the case rate payment.[10] This shift was desirable to the extent it substituted low-cost ambulatory and subacute services for high-cost inpatient care, but undesirable to the extent it encouraged the provision of additional and unnecessary services.

The most important limitation of Medicare's case rates is that the services provided by physicians to the hospitalized patient are not included in the payment. Surgeons, anesthesiologists, and other hospital-based specialists continue to be reimbursed on a fee-for-service basis for each procedure and consultation. They have no direct stake in hospital efficiency, as they are paid the same regardless of the cost of the drugs and devices used, the level of staffing, and the length of the patient's stay. Their reimbursement also does not depend on patient outcomes. There is no reward for improved transitions out of the hospital, permitting wide geographic variation in the volume and quality of postdischarge care.[11]

Policymakers and insurers are now interested in extending hospital case rates to include preadmission and postdischarge services. "Episode-of-care" payments are built around acute care interventions such as maternity, spine fusion, and kidney transplantation.[12] Episode payment can also be used to reimburse services provided to patients suffering from chronic illnesses such as diabetes or kidney failure, even when these do not center on a single major intervention.[13] A bundled fee covering a chronic illness for a specified period of time would be termed an "episode of illness" payment.

Episode payment creates incentives for caregivers to coordinate with one another, avoid unnecessary tests, select cost-effective drugs and devices, and discharge the patient promptly from the hospital. One organization receives the single payment from the insurer and is responsible for covering the bills submitted by other participants in the patient's care. The financial margin earned by the payment recipient, typically a hospital or large medical group, is what is left after the fees for ancillary providers and services have been deducted. Episode payment transfers financial responsibility from insurers to providers and thus reduces the need for insurers to second-guess provider choices through medical management.

Episodes can be analyzed in terms of their length, breadth, and depth. The length of an episode determines the range of procedures and products that will be reimbursed from the single payment, with longer episode definitions increasing the financial reward but also the administrative burden of coordination. The breadth determines how many related conditions will be covered in one episode, with broader definitions reducing the number of distinct episodes but increasing the need to adjust each one for disease severity. The depth determines which of the inputs used during the episode will be covered, with deeper episodes increasing the reward but also the risk for a judicious choice of expensive supplies and equipment.

When considering the implication of provider payment for the purchasing of medical technology, the most important dimension is episode depth. The inclusion of expensive supplies as part of the single payment motivates physicians and hospitals to seek the most efficient and affordable options. This reverses the incentives created by fee for service, which renders the providers indifferent to device costs and sometimes tilts them toward choosing the expensive options. The depth of an episode also determines whether all the caregivers will be reimbursed from the single payment. Medicare's exclusion of physician services significantly weakened its hospital case rates, since physicians determine which tests, treatments, supplies, and facilities are used for the patient.

Medicare has experimented on several occasions with deeper episode definitions that combine physician and hospital services. In 1988 it launched a demonstration initiative for coronary artery bypass surgery, paying participating hospitals a single rate covering facility and physician services; the cost of readmissions were included in the episode rate. Medicare saved $50 million from lower hospital and postdischarge care costs. Beneficiaries also saved money due to lower coinsurance.[14] More recently, Medicare piloted a bundled payment initiative for orthopedic, spine, and cardiac procedures. Physicians were paid by the participating hospitals using the Medicare fee schedule but earned a share of hospital savings from lower device costs, shorter length of stay, and other physician-influenced initiatives. The project obtained significant savings for the participating hospitals, due primarily to reduced costs for implantable devices, and hence generated additional revenues for the participating physicians.[15] CMS subsequently solicited projects that include hospital and posthospital services within one episode payment.[16] It has also begun to adjust case rate payments based on the level of ambulatory and postacute expenditures on hospitalized patients in the three days before hospital admission and thirty days after discharge.[17]

Some private insurers have developed bundled payment initiatives for acute and chronic episodes, but have found them difficult to implement. The most successful have been case rates for organ transplantation performed in regional Centers of Excellence. These Centers are often willing to contract for a single payment that covers facility charges, drugs and devices, physician services, and some elements of postdischarge care. Some insurers have sought to extend episode payment to more common procedures. For example, the Integrated Healthcare Association developed a bundled payment model for orthopedic surgery in collaboration with several insurers and hospitals in California.[18] Insurers and employers in other states sought to use bundled payment methods for chronic care. These initiatives had very limited effects, however, due to the difficulty in moving physicians and hospitals into collaborative structures that require the sharing of financial risk.[19]

POPULATION-BASED PAYMENT

Case rates and episode payments motivate physicians and hospitals to work together in selecting, delivering, and coordinating the patient's care. But it is often difficult to define when an episode begins and ends. Some patients suffer from multiple problems and it can be difficult to assign a particular test or treatment to one episode versus another. These difficulties lead to disputes as to how much is due and how it should be allocated across caregivers.

The alternative to paying for each case or episode is for the insurer to make a single payment for all the care needed over a defined period of time. The organization that receives this payment provides some of the needed services directly, using its employed physicians and owned facilities, and arranges for the provision of the other services through contractual relationships. For example, a medical group may be able to provide primary care services directly but refer patients needing complex treatments to an academic medical center. The medical group would have the incentive to increase the use of preventive and primary care services that reduce the need for hospitalization as well as to select efficient hospitals for its referrals.[20]

Population-based payments shift the financial risk normally borne by the health insurer onto the health care organization. This is desirable to the extent the caregivers can prevent the incidence and manage the cost of care more effectively than the insurer. But it places great strains on the organization's financial and administrative capabilities, and has proven too risky for many medical groups and hospitals. Some forms of population-based payment therefore restrict the provider's financial responsibility to primary care services, and are referred to as "medical home" payment methods. Others cover the services of specialist as well as generalist physicians but exclude hospital services, and are referred to as "professional services" capitation. Some initiatives limit the provider's financial responsibility to a particular condition, such as mental health or cancer care, and are referred to as "specialty" capitation.

The exclusion of particular providers or conditions from population-based payment requires the establishment of boundaries between covered and noncovered services, precisely the problem that plagues case rates and episode payments. The alternative is to include all providers and services under a single payment but share the financial risk among several parties. The health care organization can agree with the insurer on a target level of expenditure for a population, based on expected trends in epidemiology and technology. If expenditures fall below this target, the savings are shared between the insurer and the providers. If expenditures exceed the target, the losses could be shared or assumed solely by the insurer.

Insurers and providers that use population-based methods of payment favor versions that cover a broad set of services but limit the degree of risk transfer. The parties negotiate expenditure targets for the coming year covering all or most clinical services. Differences between actual and expected expenditures are shared between all the parties to the agreement, with more sophisticated physician and hospital organizations accepting a large percentage of gains and losses while less sophisticated entities leave more of the risk and reward with the insurer.[21]

Population-based payments need to be adjusted for severity of illness lest providers that attract patients needing more expensive services be penalized. Contemporary payment methods combine prospective adjustments for patient characteristics that can be measured prior to the payment period with retrospective adjustments for factors measured during the payment period. They may provide supplemental payments for especially complex procedures, using case rates or fee for service.

ADJUSTING PAYMENTS TO PROMOTE INNOVATION

Case rates, episode payments, and population-based payments reward the adoption of clinical technologies that reduce the cost of care. If a physician practice or hospital selects a cheaper test or treatment or improves the efficiency of its processes, it keeps the savings rather than seeing them accrue to the insurer. A dollar saved is a dollar earned.

But many important new technologies increase costs. When paid on a prospective basis, providers face the temptation to avoid these technologies and the patients who need them. This, in turn, reduces the incentives for manufacturers to invest in research and development. It is imperative that new payment methods be adjusted to account for new cost-increasing supplies and equipment so as not to discourage the adoption and, indirectly, the development of innovative technologies.

The adjustment of payment methods is illustrated in the evolution of payment for catheter-based treatment of coronary artery disease. The evolution of this treatment, which combined breakthrough and incremental innovations, required major changes in Medicare's case rate payments for hospitals.[22]

Prior to 1980, occlusion of the coronary arteries was treated by drugs, which were of limited effectiveness, or by bypass surgery, which was traumatic for patients with comorbidities. In 1977, angioplasty was introduced as an alternative to surgery. Angioplasty threads a narrow inflatable balloon through the femoral artery into the patient's heart, where it is inflated to push open closed arteries. Unfortunately, the arteries frequently shrink back after the balloon is removed, either abruptly in the catheterization laboratory or after the patient is discharged from the hospital. In 1987 cardiologists introduced coronary stents to remedy this often-disastrous complication. Narrow wire mesh scaffolds were inserted as part of the angioplasty procedure and left in the artery after the balloon was removed.

Stents significantly reduced the need for revision angioplasty or surgery, and in 1994 they received FDA authorization for routine use. However, the stent devices themselves added thousands of dollars to the hospital's cost of performing the angioplasty procedure. Hospitals argued for an increase in Medicare's case rate payment. They received vigorous support from the stent manufacturers, who were understandably concerned that their customers would not enthusiastically adopt money-losing technologies. CMS conducted a study of actual costs incurred in the angioplasty procedures, and found wide variation across hospitals, from $9,000 to $45,000. It declined to increase the payment rate, because the price of the stent itself fell within the range of allowable costs. In 1998, however, CMS assigned stent-based angioplasty procedures to a new DRG category, with a payment $2,120 above the rate for angioplasty procedures that did not use stents.

Angioplasty with stents diffused rapidly and displaced drug treatment and bypass surgery for many patients. However, the new procedure was plagued by restenosis, the gradual narrowing of the arteries after angioplasty caused by the growth of new tissue in and around the stent scaffolds. Clinical guidelines recommended the use of anti-inflammatory medications to accompany coronary stents and thereby limit restenosis. In 2003 manufacturers received FDA market approval for stents infused with slow-release anti-inflammatory drugs.[23] The manufacturers priced these drug-eluting stents at significantly higher levels than their bare metal predecessors, again leading to hospital calls for payment increases. CMS assigned angioplasty with drug-eluting stents to yet another DRG category, with a rate $1,500 higher than the rate for angioplasty using bare metal devices. This case rate increase was below the average price of drug-eluting stents but moderated the adverse financial impact on hospital budgets.

The experience with coronary stents led Medicare to institute a formal process for exempting high-value innovations from case rates, which is called the new technology add-on payment.[24] Medical technologies seeking to qualify must face severe financial barriers to adoption due to high costs, and must offer a meaningful new option to patients who are unresponsive to other treatments. Eligible devices must reduce patient pain, bleeding, or other quantifiable symptoms, device-related complications, disease recurrence, surgical revision, hospital readmission, rehabilitation time, or mortality. To be eligible for new payment, diagnostic tests must permit accurate diagnosis of a condition whose treatment can be improved based on the improved diagnosis; improved diagnosis without improvement in treatment is not sufficient. The supplemental payment is set at 50 percent of the eligible technology's price in order to give hospitals the incentive to negotiate discounts with manufacturers, employ the technology in an efficient manner, and adopt lower-price alternatives as they emerge. Hospital case rates in European nations also feature supplemental payments for high-cost technologies, including drug-eluting stents.[25]

Private insurers could and should follow Medicare's lead in adjusting payments for changes in medical technology. Health care providers should be paid adequately for quality-improving new technologies, even if they increase costs. However, add-on payments should not be an open-ended reimbursement for any new product, regardless of its appropriateness or price. Supplemental payments should be limited to technologies that are used within evidence-based treatment protocols. They should be paid at rates that motivate providers to negotiate discounts and to switch to cheaper products as they emerge. The period of time during which a technology receives supplemental payment should be used to collect data on the efficient cost of the product and the processes within which it is used. These data will permit an updating of the base payment rate and the subsequent elimination of the new technology payment supplement. And most obviously, the supplemental payments should be of limited duration; no technology is new forever.

CONCLUSION

New methods of provider payment are important but, by themselves, cannot ensure the efficient use of medical technology. Insurers can create financial incentives through payment mechanisms, but providers must develop the capabilities for technology assessment, procurement, and use. As this occurs, hospitals and their physicians will constitute the third stage, after FDA market regulation and insurer coverage and reimbursement, in the purchasing of medical technology.

4

The Hospital as Purchaser

Hospitals historically competed for patient admissions by competing for physician affiliations, using technology as the preferred weapon in what became known as the "medical arms race."[1] Doctors wanted new and better facilities, equipment, staffing, and supplies, and the hospital provided them. The medical arms race accelerated the diffusion and thereby the development of medical technology. Rapid adoption provided manufacturers the revenues needed to sustain investments in research. Hospitals also served as a locus for innovation, encouraging physicians to experiment with new designs, materials, and procedures. But there can be too much of a good thing. The medical arms race spurred the duplication of clinical equipment and capabilities among hospitals, undermining the regionalization of complex procedures into high-volume and high-quality centers. It focused hospitals on the number rather than the appropriateness of the services provided.

Hospitals now are under pressure to improve the efficiency of their services. Medicare is pressuring hospitals to do more with less. Private insurers are narrowing their networks in pursuit of price discounts. Bundled methods of payment reward processes that reduce costs. Hospitals are challenged to adopt and use technology in ways fundamentally different from the arms race of years past.

This chapter analyzes the hospital as a purchaser of medical technology. It begins with a look backward at the medical arms race, describes the resulting pushback from insurers, and examines hospital technology strategy in the new era of resource constraints. It highlights technology assessment, procurement, pricing, and utilization, the key dimensions of purchasing. The focus is on principles and widespread practices; detailed examples from individual hospitals are provided in the subsequent chapter.

THE MEDICAL ARMS RACE

The community hospital was traditionally structured to serve the needs of an independent physician community, providing the beds, staffing, supplies, and equipment required to treat patients with conditions too complex to be handled in the office. Indeed, observers often referred to the hospital as the "physician's workshop."[2] Doctors were not employed by the hospital but owned their private practices, which functioned like small businesses or professional partnerships.[3] They often admitted patients to more than one hospital facility, depending on each individual's clinical condition, geographic residence, and type of insurance.

The hospital served the physician but the physician also served the hospital. Most obviously, the doctors decided where to admit their patients, and hence were the principal source of the hospital's volume and revenue. Some patients came into the facility through the emergency department, but the majority acquiesced in the recommendations of the physician with whom they had an ongoing affiliation. Hospitals cultivated physician loyalty and, in communities with many facilities, competed for it. Professional ethics and regulatory strictures prevented hospitals from directly compensating physicians for admitting patients, but competition for physician loyalty was vigorous nonetheless. Hospitals offered free parking, doctors' lounges, help with administrative chores, and other amenities. More important were the clinical facilities, equipment, and supplies offered for the physician's use. Hospitals built state-of-the-art operating rooms and catheterization laboratories, created centers for oncology and neurology, acquired the latest generation of laboratory and imaging equipment, and offered the full range of implantable medical devices.

The costs of competition were passed from hospitals to insurers and, beyond them, to the employers, governmental agencies, and individuals who paid insurance premiums. The more the hospitals spent, the more they earned. Medicare reimbursed hospitals based on operating costs, which rewarded facilities that aggressively adopted expensive technologies. With the imposition of case rates in the 1980s, Medicare began constraining the cost of hospital care, but continued to reward technologies that increased service volume and complexity. Private insurers lagged behind their public counterpart, continuing to reimburse hospitals based on list prices and daily rates.

The technology-based competition for physician affiliations fueled an explosion in health care costs. If one hospital in a community acquired an expensive imaging modality, nearby facilities rushed to purchase a similar or equally appealing technology.[4] This expansion and duplication of medical technology

increased the costs of care. Whereas competition in most industries leads to reductions in costs, hospitals in markets with vigorous competition exhibited substantially higher expenditures per
patient than otherwise similar hospitals in markets with less
competition.[5]

The medical arms race benefited the technology industry.
Manufacturers knew that hospitals could not credibly threaten
to reject their products, regardless of the price, for fear of antag-
onizing physicians. Everyone knew the hospitals could pass the
bill to the insurer. The arms race also offered important benefits
to patients. The improvements in health status during recent
decades have been due in part to improvements in lifestyle, such
as smoking reduction, and in part to improved primary care,
such as drugs to lower blood pressure. A meaningful part of the
improvement derives, however, from hospital-based diagnostic
and therapeutic technologies.[6]

PHYSICIAN PREFERENCE ITEMS

The medical arms race was particularly vigorous for services
that were expanding, profitable, and prestigious, such as cardiac
surgery and interventional cardiology.[7] For example, hospitals
in markets with competitors already supporting cardiac catheterization and surgery facilities were over twice as likely to perform angioplasty and bypass surgery as otherwise similar hospitals in less competitive markets. In competitive markets, each
physician specialist was responsible for millions of dollars in
hospital revenue each year. Hospitals were not going to kill the
goose that laid the golden egg. They were especially reluctant to
question physician preferences in service lines that were adding
new procedures and expanding the volume of admissions. This

pattern was precisely opposite the one that would be desired. In a well-designed health system, hospitals in markets that lack advanced services would be more likely to initiate new services, while facilities in well-served markets would be less likely.

Implantable medical devices differ from more humble components of the hospital's supply chain, such as bandages and surgical gowns. Physicians do not have brand preferences for clinical commodities, but allow the hospital to negotiate with suppliers based on price. Physicians have very specific preferences, however, for spine fusion implants, cardiac defibrillators, drug-eluting stents, and other high-performance implantable devices. These preferences change the dynamics of purchasing.

Physicians sometimes prefer specific device brands for clinical reasons. There may be meaningful performance differences across products within a broad therapeutic category, and physicians will want to make the selection based on the best fit with their clinical skills and their patients' needs. Different orthopedic implants require different instruments and methods of insertion, for example, and surgeons typically learn to work with one product line and stick to it rather than undergo retraining on a new one. Cardiac rhythm management devices are connected to the heart's electrical circuitry with different types of lead wires. The clinical evidence shows few differences in patient outcomes across competing products, but an individual cardiologist may achieve better outcomes with a familiar brand.

Physician brand preferences are also based on financial inducements. Manufacturers recognize that each specialist represents a major source of sales and target their marketing efforts accordingly. Physicians are paid patent royalties if they help develop a device, consulting fees if they give feedback on its performance, speaking honoraria if they promote the device at professional meetings, and expense-paid trips to medical education meetings where new devices are presented. These payments implicitly reward brand loyalty. Physicians receive patent fees even if their contribution is minimal, consulting fees even if they just fill out a brief survey, speaking fees even for casual dinner remarks, and expense-paid travel even to events with minimal scientific content.

The physician's preferences are also strengthened by the manner in which devices are distributed. The physician's selection among brands, models, and sizes must often be performed in the course of a medical procedure, based on a last-minute assessment of the patient's condition. Device representatives are usually present in the operating room and cardiac catheterization laboratory to aid with the procedure, giving them an opportunity to suggest their preferred products. Physicians often develop personal relationships with particular vendors, and insist on access to their representative's product line. In these contexts, the hospital lacks any ability to manage its supply chain. It is not a purchaser, but merely an entity that reimburses manufacturers. The physician, and not the hospital, is the customer.

For many years hospitals were unable to escape the medical arms race. Surgeons could threaten to move their admissions elsewhere if their favorite brand of device were not available. Most were indifferent to the hospitals' budgetary challenges and resisted hospital efforts to manage devices in a manner similar to other supplies. Individual surgeons often did not want to coordinate with other members of the medical staff on the choice of implants, and opposed requirements for new devices to be approved by a technology assessment committee. Physicians did not want to disclose their consulting relationships with drug and device manufacturers or, for that matter, with clinical laboratories, surgery centers, and imaging facilities. They certainly did not want anyone to limit those lucrative relationships.

Hospitals negotiated contracts with insurers that allowed them to pass on the inflated costs of medical technology. Many hospital contracts with insurers explicitly "carved" implantable devices out from the basic payment. The hospital submitted an additional claim for reimbursement for the device. Some hospitals converted device costs into a new source of profits, charging insurers at rates significantly above what the hospital paid the device manufacturer. In their turn, the insurers passed the costs of medical devices to their subscribers. For the medical technology industry, it was a field of dreams.

PUSHBACK

Unsustainable trends cannot be sustained, even in health care. There were ever more tests and treatments, prescribed by physicians enjoying financial inducements, purchased by hospitals eager for growth, and reimbursed by insurers indifferent to cost; the only wonder was that expenditures did not rise faster than they did. Health care expenditures grew at an annual rate several percentage points faster than the economy as a whole, decade after decade, absorbing an ever-growing share of public and private budgets and requiring ever-greater borrowing to finance the ever-greater spending.

The first serious pushback against the expansion of medical technology came from Medicare. The public entity updates its case rates each year based on changes in the hospital sector's underlying rate of cost growth. But it must also consider the consequences for the federal budget. It implicitly slows payment updates as it perceives the budgetary environment to become more difficult. Over time, Medicare's reimbursements began to lag behind the hospitals' costs, squeezing contribution margins and deepening financial losses for publicly insured patients.[8] The decline in Medicare margins was especially problematic in technology-intensive hospital service lines that had historically been the most profitable. For example, Medicare margins for cardiac services fell nationally from 50 percent in 2001 to 38 percent in 2010.[9]

The squeeze on Medicare margins did not immediately force changes in hospital technology strategy. The first response was to increase prices to private insurers. Insurers were able to slow the growth in hospital prices during the 1990s by contracting selectively with a limited number of facilities in each market, trading higher patient volume for price discounts.[10] This strategy presumed that there existed sufficient numbers of independent hospitals in each market. But the hospital industry began to reduce its capacity and thereby its vulnerability to competition. Between 1991 and 2011, the number of community hospitals in the United States declined from 5,342 to 4,973.[11] Many of the surviving institutions reduced their capacity. The number of staffed beds declined from 922,822 to 825,966 in 2001 and 797,403 in 2011. Population continued to expand, and so the ratio of beds per 1,000 persons shrank by 21 percent from 1991 to 2001 and by 30 percent from 1991 to 2011.[12]

The hospital industry also became less competitive due to mergers and acquisitions. Independent hospitals began to merge with neighboring institutions, insisting that health plans contract with all members of the merged system rather than pit individual facilities against one another. Hospital chains began to acquire facilities in markets where they were already strong, divesting facilities in communities where they lacked critical mass.[13]

Consolidation was successful in the short run but merely delayed the hospitals' day of reckoning. The employers who paid the insurers' premiums saw an ever-increasing share of total employee compensation diverted to health benefits, without commensurate improvements in productivity. They began adopting benefit designs that required more consumer cost sharing at the time of receiving care. The pushback was addressed not merely at overall hospital costs but at the specifics of the technology procurement process. Leading media sources began shedding unfavorable light on the financial incentives offered to physicians for using high-cost tests and treatments. In 2007 the US Department of Justice required manufacturers of orthopedic devices to post online the financial sums they paid out to each physician each year. The numbers were shocking.[14] It became evident that many doctors were earning consulting fees in the hundreds of thousands of dollars each year, substantially more than they were earning from their clinical skills. The initial disclosures increased the public's demand for more. The Affordable Care Act of 2010 included "sunshine" provisions that require manufacturers of pharmaceuticals and medical devices to annually post their payments to all types of physicians, not merely to orthopedic surgeons.[15]

It is but a short step from mandated disclosure to a regulatory ban. Research conducted during the 1970s and 1980s had documented excessive use of laboratory and radiology tests by physicians who held a financial investment in the technologies.[16] Federal legislation passed in 1989 and 1993 banned the referral of Medicare patients to clinical laboratories, diagnostic imaging facilities, and ambulatory surgery centers in which physicians held an ownership interest.[17] The Affordable Care Act extended this ban to hospitals, with the greatest impact being felt by specialized orthopedic and cardiology facilities. Specialty hospitals that were already functioning could continue but new facilities would be excluded from Medicare reimbursement and hence would not be financially viable.

The pushback by insurers, employers, and governmental agencies against the medical arms race has forced hospitals to reconsider their technology strategy. While physicians will always want new facilities and equipment, the hospital no longer can assume that the resulting costs will be reimbursed. Hospitals are becoming more discriminating in their methods of technology assessment, the manner by which they contract with manufacturers, the prices they are willing to pay, and the manner by which they incorporate new technology into their clinical processes.

TECHNOLOGY ASSESSMENT

Hospitals traditionally did not assess the performance of the technologies used by their medical staff. This hands-off policy stemmed from the institution's desire to respect the clinical autonomy of highly trained professionals and, more prosaically, from its fear of alienating the source of patient admissions. Weak assessment led to indiscriminate adoption. Without an ability to compare products based on price and performance, hospitals had little ability to contract selectively with manufacturers and effectively manage their supply chain. The proliferation of products added further complexity to technology acquisition, inventory, staffing, and replacement.

In the new era of constrained revenues, the adoption of technology without rigorous assessment is no longer viable. Leading institutions are establishing technology assessment committees comprising practicing physicians and senior management. These committees assess new diagnostic tests, imaging modalities, implantable devices, and other technologies in terms of whether they improve outcomes for patients and, if so, whether the incremental benefits are worth the incremental costs.[18] In some ways they are analogous to the "Pharmacy and Therapeutics" committees maintained by insurers to assess drugs for coverage and reimbursement. Membership in a hospital committee includes specialists who use technology most intensively; subcommittees with additional members can be formed for particularly complex technologies. Practicing physicians who wish to champion particular devices can do so in front of the committee, marshaling the available evidence, but must disclose potential conflicts of interest. In the past hospitals sometimes found they were obliged to pay for a new device after a physician had already administered it to a patient, without prior notification. Now equipment and supplies that have not been approved by the technology assessment committee will not be reimbursed by the hospital, but must be considered a charitable donation to the facility by the manufacturer.

Hospital technology assessment committees serve three important purposes. They support the hospital's adoption of breakthrough innovations, its supply chain for established products, and its cultural alignment with physicians.

For breakthrough innovations that have no direct substitutes, the focus of a technology assessment committee is to help the hospital decide which services to offer and which to avoid. Not every hospital can provide every service and perform every procedure. Breakthrough technologies often require substantial financial investments to acquire equipment, design supportive facilities, attract specialized staff, and monitor clinical outcomes.

Each technology needs to be assessed in light of the hospital's organizational capabilities. The technology assessment committee needs to answer questions that are complex both clinically and economically. Just how important are the incremental benefits offered by the new technology? What are likely to be the total costs, including acquisition, facilities, and staffing? Will the hospital have sufficient volumes to justify the investment? Hospitals have only limited evidence with which to answer these difficult questions. Some adopt a new technology in the face of uncertainty, monitor performance for several years, and then formally reconsider adoption, in a manner analogous to the FDA's policy of postmarket surveillance and Medicare's policy of coverage with evidence development.

For incremental innovations that compete with already available products, the technology assessment committee focuses on comparative rather than absolute performance. Is the new product meaningfully better than those already in use? Is there evidence of reduced complications and readmissions, shorter length of stay, better functional ability, reduced discomfort and pain, or other meaningful outcomes? Is it more expensive? Do we need to adopt all variants of a technology or can we meet our needs with just a few?

Technology assessment committees can serve an important cultural role. When they attract meaningful physician participation, they provide a context for discussing quality based on evidence rather than on perception. Of equal importance, the committee's deliberations can legitimize for physicians the consideration of cost in clinical decision-making. Traditionally physicians paid little attention to price and, indeed, felt that a concern for cost would violate their professional obligation to the patients. Hospital committees do not conduct formal cost-effectiveness analyses, but do consider the budgetary impact of new technologies. A vote by a physician-led committee can stiffen the backbone of managers confronted with demands by individual doctors to acquire new technologies despite a lack of supportive evidence.

TECHNOLOGY PROCUREMENT

The process of procurement varies across different medical technologies, depending on the scale of the purchase and on whether there exist multiple vendors. Major imaging modalities, therapeutic radiology equipment, and other high-cost equipment must be incorporated into the hospital's capital planning and budgeting cycle, and often rely on the technology committee primarily for clinical rather than economic expertise. Drugs, implantable devices, and laboratory tests are purchased out of the institution's operating budget, however, and are analyzed by the technology committee as part of supply chain management.

Hospitals with nonaligned medical staffs cannot contract selectively with technology suppliers, especially when under competitive pressures to be all things to all doctors. But as hospitals develop a stronger medical staff alignment, either by employing physicians or by developing partnerships with medical groups, they are able to pursue a more effective process of technology procurement.

The dominant hospital procurement strategy is to contract with only two or three, but not all, of the available medical device manufacturers.[19] A reduction in the number of suppliers permits the hospital to promise greater volume and higher margins to each one. It reduces the costs of product distribution, since device representatives cover a larger number of procedures at a smaller number of facilities. The hospital has fewer suppliers to monitor, device types to retain in inventory, and training sessions for nurses and operating room technicians.

Limiting the number of technology suppliers is a good strategy, but limiting it to one supplier is not. It is difficult for a single device manufacturer to offer the full range of products needed by a hospital's medical staff. It is also difficult for a hospital to predict which manufacturer will be most innovative in future years. Most importantly, exclusive contracting creates a potential monopoly from what was formerly a competitive market. Once all the hospital's physicians have agreed to use one supplier's product line, and once the hospital's inventory, accounting, and management systems have adapted accordingly, it is difficult to switch to a competitor. Physicians need to be convinced that the new product line is effective clinically, the operating room staff needs to be retrained, inventories need to be returned, and the accumulated experience working with the supplier's systems is lost. The original supplier understands this, of course, and can raise prices accordingly when the contract comes up for renewal. What initially appeared to be a cost-effective sole-source relationship may turn out to be a costly locked-in relationship.

Once a hospital has focused its device purchases on a small number of suppliers, it becomes feasible to extend the term of the contracts. Longer terms reduce the transaction costs of complex negotiations. They commit buyers and sellers to finding ways to sustain the relationship even as the environment changes, recognizing that the costs of a termination would be high to both sides. Only when there is some guarantee of continuity does it make economic sense to invest in the relationship, sharing information on product performance, organizational strategies, and likely regulatory changes. Long-term relationships foster trust and reduce the need to monitor each interaction, recognizing that an idiosyncratic profit or loss on one product can be offset later. In the language of organizational economics, the procurement process can evolve from a short term "spot contract," where price is the only consideration, to a longer term "relational contract," where data sharing, collaborative planning, and nonlitigious dispute resolution mechanisms are important.[20] Needless to say, trust only goes so far; it is also important to verify. Contracts need to be reassessed every three to five years in light of new opportunities in the environment.

TECHNOLOGY PRICING

The hospital supply chain contains thousands of items, the prices of which need to be negotiated in light of their clinical value, the prices of comparable products, the volume of purchases, and the conditions of sale and service. Hospitals and manufacturers must find a way to reduce the number of discrete prices that must be adjudicated, lest the haggling overwhelm managerial capabilities and envenom organizational relationships.

Manufacturers create a schedule of list prices for each product and component, and are typically willing to offer percentage discounts to favored customers. From the point of view of most hospitals, however, list prices are an unattractive basis for negotiations. The rates embody what the manufacturer feels the least sophisticated part of the market will pay, rather than being linked in any systematic fashion to product performance or patient outcomes. List prices contain no information on what competing manufacturers are willing to accept for comparable products. And there is nothing stopping a manufacturer that offers a 25 percent discount off its list prices from then raising those prices by 25 percent.

Most hospitals are moving toward some form of pricing matrix, which assigns products to categories based on their expected clinical uses and then sets a maximum price for each category.[21] The price cap is based on preliminary bids or prevailing trends in the market. It must be high enough to encourage multiple manufacturers to bid for the business but low enough to create incentives for discounts. Some hospitals use a product matrix to solicit bids for each category of device, and then extend contracts to all suppliers willing to set prices below the cap. This any-willing-vendor strategy retains a large number of suppliers while keeping prices under control, but focuses excessively on price to the exclusion of service. It also subjects the hospital to the risk that manufacturers will substitute lower-quality products within each matrix category. Other hospitals use a product matrix to eliminate the least cooperative vendors, and then explore contractual possibilities with two or three firms that offer prices below the cap while providing valuable technical, distribution, and inventory services.[22]

The most difficult dimension of pricing strategy concerns rates for new devices and modifications of existing devices, as these often fall outside the established product matrix. This is of particular concern for clinical domains such as spine fusion, which are undergoing rapid evolution in product designs but lack definitive clinical studies. Some manufacturers are willing to offer attractive rates on established products but then insist that new items be reimbursed at list price. This can be acceptable to a hospital if the number of new items is small and the criteria for defining a device as new are clearly established. But new technology exemptions open the door to opportunistic tactics by distributors who can define modified products as new even if the changes do not affect patient outcomes. Some hospitals require that a new device be certified by the technology assessment committee as offering meaningful new benefits before being reimbursed at a rate higher than the previous model, regardless of the changes in design, materials, or mode of administration.

From the perspective of the manufacturer, the device is the product and its price must cover the cost of development, manufacturing, and distribution. From the perspective of the hospital, however, the procedure is the product and the device is only one component. The price of the device must not be so high as to eliminate the hospital's margin on the case. To the extent hospitals have strong leverage and can carve the device cost out of the insurer's base reimbursement formula, they can be sympathetic to manufacturers' views concerning device price adequacy. But for Medicare patients, hospitals cannot carve out device costs. Some hospitals seek to negotiate device prices based on the patient care revenues they obtain. This can be done by limiting prices for particular devices to a percentage of the reimbursement obtained by the hospital for the procedure.

At the end of the day, high prices are good for device manufacturers but bad for hospitals, while low prices are good for hospitals but bad for manufacturers. Manufacturers have a minimum device price they must achieve in order to cover their costs, and cannot accept lower rates except for strategic reasons. Hospitals have a maximum device price they cannot exceed, given the procedure revenues they expect, and cannot pay higher rates except for special reasons. There may be a considerable range between the manufacturer's minimum and the hospital's maximum price. Here bargaining sophistication proves its value. There is no reason to expect that the prices paid for the same device by different hospitals will always be the same. Bargaining outcomes depend on the volume of sales, the extent to which practicing physicians comply with the hospital's contracts, and the ability of a multihospital chain to ensure volumes and compliance across its facilities.

Quality and cost depend not merely on the characteristics of a medical technology, but on the appropriateness of the procedure and the site of care, the preparation of the patient prior to surgery, the skill of the clinical team, the avoidance of complications, and the coordination of care after discharge. Improvement in technology purchasing is thus only the first step in the improvement of the hospital's technology-intensive service lines.

The most expensive moment in health care is the extra minute in the operating room. Surgical and catheterization suites are filled with costly equipment and staffed by expensive physicians, nurses, and technicians. Each procedure is a major source of revenue, and the number of cases that can be performed per day has enormous implications for the hospital's financial well-being. Even when the hospital is paid on a capitation basis, efficient use of the operating room is essential to holding down the capacity needed for the covered population of patients.

Clinical procedures often resemble continuous flow processes in other industries. Principles of lean manufacturing, which minimizes unnecessary use of staff and supplies, can be applied to the operating room, as can principles of just-in-time inventory and continuous quality improvement. Improvements require the standardization of processes to reduce variance and achieve performance benchmarks. It requires the systematic collection of data on which patient received which device for which purpose. Ideally these data are embedded in a registry for subsequent analyses. Better patient preparation, operating room scheduling, and staff coordination increase the number of cases that can be treated per day.

Medical devices have short product cycles, and hence pose serious challenges to hospital inventory management. No facility wants to stock stents, defibrillators, and other devices that might be obsolete before they are inserted in a patient and paid for by an insurer. Orthopedic implants come in many shapes and sizes and must be fitted to a particular patient during the operation itself. Hospitals have historically relied on representatives of the device firms to bring products with them, rather than maintaining inventory in the facility itself. This delegation of inventory management shifts to the manufacturer the financial risk of product obsolescence. However, it also strengthens the bond between the device representative and the surgeon, and correspondingly weakens the surgeon's bond with the hospital. Some hospitals therefore stock commonly used devices directly. Others are training employees to assist the surgeon with device inventory and instruments, eliminating the organization's reliance on vendor representatives for noncomplicated cases.

Principles of continuous quality improvement can be applied to the process of care after the patient has completed the acute intervention. The process of recovery and rehabilitation requires the coordination of staff nurses, physical therapists, social workers, and occupational therapists, plus an often-complex mix of antibiotics, pain medications, and follow-up tests. Efficiency can be improved significantly if management analyzes each subprocess in terms of its relation to the others, both temporally and clinically, eliminating duplication and identifying services that need not be provided at all. The goal is to accelerate the patient's return to full functioning, avoid post-surgical complications, and reduce the chance of readmission.

The recovery process in the hospital needs to be coordinated with recovery processes after discharge. Planning for discharge ideally begins when the patient is admitted, or even before, to help ensure that family and community supports will be available when needed. Depending on the severity of the patient's condition, postdischarge placement could be made with a rehabilitation hospital, skilled nursing facility, or professional home care services.

The efficient purchasing of medical technology is key to the success of the hospital, but the efficient delivery of unnecessary treatments is not. It is always a struggle for hospitals to assess the appropriateness of the care provided by their affiliated physicians, due to the profitability of the procedures and management's reluctance to interfere with professional judgment. Nevertheless, hospitals recognize they are under scrutiny from regulators, insurers, and journalists. Capitation and other bundled methods of payment reduce the incentives for overtreatment but create new worries about undertreatment. Leading hospitals address appropriateness directly by reviewing the criteria used by their medical staff. As they seek to contract selectively with hospitals, insurers now expect Centers of Excellence to commit to appropriateness as well as to quality and efficiency.

CONCLUSION

The medical arms race has not ended. Hospitals continue to compete for physicians and patients by providing state-of-the-art facilities, equipment, and devices. But after years of acquiring each new technology, regardless of cost, hospitals no longer contract with every vendor, turn a blind eye to questionable marketing practices, and pay any price demanded. Hospitals are evolving from passive payers into active purchasers of medical technology.

5

Organizational Capabilities for Technology Purchasing

The transformation of the hospital is one of the most important developments in the market for medical technology, but individual facilities vary in their capabilities to serve as effective purchasers. They seek to hone skills in technology assessment, develop contractual relationships with suppliers, negotiate acceptable prices, and coordinate the patient's course of care. Scale and scope are essential, as is the institution's alignment with its medical staff. Physicians historically enjoyed the medical arms race, playing one hospital off against another to obtain the latest equipment and facilities, and some still prefer the traditional style of practice. But physicians now face increasing demands for performance improvement at the same time professional fees are under pressure, and many seek to work more closely with their local hospital.

The previous chapter analyzed the challenges facing all hospitals as purchasers of medical technology. This chapter highlights the variation among hospitals, with an emphasis on the orthopedics and cardiology service lines. The chapter begins by describing five hospitals that were selected for in-depth study. Each institution's purchasing strategy is analyzed in terms of technology assessment, number of contracted suppliers, contract duration, ability to ensure physician cooperation, and potential for partnership with technology firms. The chapter then examines device pricing for standardized products, for new technologies, and as a percentage of the hospital's patient care revenue. Hospital efforts to improve the use of medical technology are described in terms of surgical processes, postsurgical patient recovery, discharge planning, and assessment of treatment alternatives.

HOSPITALS AND PHYSICIANS

Insights concerning hospital structure, physician alignment, and technology purchasing can best be obtained from case studies, since only these provide sufficient detail and the ability to pursue the "why" behind the "what" in organizational behavior. The case studies used here focused on five hospital systems that together dominate one major geographic market, thereby avoiding the influences exerted by regional differences in regulation, competition, and the cost of living.

The hospital systems include St. Joseph Health, Tenet Healthcare, Hoag Memorial Presbyterian, MemorialCare Health System, and Kaiser Permanente. Together they dominate the market in Orange County, a suburban area in Southern California with approximately five million residents.[1] One major hospital facility was selected for extensive analysis from within each multihospital system. Interviews were conducted with the chief executive, financial, and medical officers; managers responsible for operating rooms, supply chain, technology assessment, and insurer contracting; and practicing surgeons and physicians. The case studies were conducted between 2010 and 2013. Characteristics of the hospitals, the health systems to which they belong, their medical staffs, and their physician alignment are presented in table 2.

St. Joseph Health is a fourteen-hospital system with three large inpatient facilities, several aligned physician organizations, and a variety of ambulatory care centers in Orange County. St. Jude Medical Center, the most prominent of the system's facilities, has an ownership relationship with the Heritage Healthcare multispecialty medical group, which accounts for 85 percent of the hospital's admissions. The other hospitals in St. Joseph Health have weaker physician relationships. Their medical staffs continue to practice in small groups, are less closely aligned with the hospital system, and frequently admit patients to competing hospitals. It is difficult for St. Joseph Health to coordinate technology purchasing across its entire system, even though it is well aligned with physicians at St. Jude.

Fountain Valley Regional Hospital is a flagship facility for the investor-owned Tenet Healthcare, which at the time of the study had four facilities in Orange County and forty-nine nationally. The medical staff is fragmented among numerous independent practices, none of which is formally affiliated with the hospital. Coordination among the physicians at different hospitals within the Tenet system is also limited. Most physicians who admit patients to Fountain Valley also admit to competing facilities, with the choice of hospital often depending on the patient's insurance coverage.

Hoag Orthopedic Institute (HOI) is a specialty hospital jointly owned by Hoag Memorial Presbyterian hospital and two

TABLE 2

Characteristics of hospitals and their medical staffs

	St. Jude Medical Center	Fountain Valley Regional Hospital	Hoag Orthopedic Institute	Long Beach Memorial Medical Center	Kaiser Permanente Irvine Medical Center
Number of staffed beds in hospital	347	293	70	420	150
Number of hospitals in national or local system	14	49	2	4	28
Ability to coordinate among hospitals in system	Moderate	Low	High	Low	High
Characteristics of medical staff	1 large multispecialty group	Many small practices	2 large orthopedic groups	Many small practices	1 large multispecialty group
Patients from partner medical groups (%)					
Orthopedics	100	0	100	0	100
Spine surgery	85	0	100	0	100
Cardiac procedures	85	0	Not applicable	0	100
Staff physicians admit to competing hospitals	None	Many	Some	Many	None

orthopedic surgical groups. The larger Hoag medical staff mostly comprises small practices without close alignment to the hospital, but Hoag has long had a strong affiliation with its orthopedic surgeons. In 2010 Hoag and the surgeons created the joint venture including a specialty hospital and two ambulatory surgery centers, bringing in a surgical group that had previously been a competitor. The surgeons are financially and culturally aligned with the joint venture, and only few admit patients to competing hospitals. Most spine surgery procedures, however, continue to be performed by nonaffiliated orthopedists and neurosurgeons.

The MemorialCare Health System encompasses four facilities, including the flagship Long Beach Memorial Medical Center. The dispersion of the Memorial facilities has hampered coordination, especially for physician-oriented initiatives, since the medical staffs do not overlap geographically and are fragmented among small practices. MemorialCare has begun acquiring medical groups but its admissions for technology-intensive services continue to come from independent practices. Many of the specialists and surgeons at Long Beach Memorial also admit patients to competing hospitals.

Kaiser Permanente is an integrated delivery system comprising a health insurance plan, regional medical groups, and twenty-eight hospitals in California and Oregon. It has a strong presence in Orange County, with two inpatient facilities, numerous ambulatory clinics, and one large medical group. Within the county, orthopedic surgery is regionalized to the Irvine Medical Center, while spine surgery and interventional cardiology are regionalized to other facilities. Kaiser has an exclusive partnership with the Permanente Medical Group in southern California. All admissions to the Irvine Medical Center come from Permanente physicians, and Permanente physicians do not admit patients to competing hospitals except when Kaiser has negotiated a contractual relationship for specialized services.

TECHNOLOGY ASSESSMENT AND PROCUREMENT

The five hospital systems differ in their approaches to technology assessment and contracting, in turn influencing their relationships with the manufacturers and distributors of medical devices. Table 3 highlights strategies for artificial joint replacements; similar patterns prevail for implantable devices related to spine surgery and interventional cardiology.

The five facilities and their larger hospital systems have committees charged with the assessment of new technology, but physician participation and compliance vary widely. Technology assessment is strongest at Hoag, due to the interest of the surgeon owners in all aspects of hospital efficiency, and at Kaiser Irvine, due to its long-standing partnership with the Permanente Medical Group. Kaiser Permanente maintains perhaps the most sophisticated technology assessment process in the nation, since it has system-wide and physician-led committees for each major specialty and service line. The doctors, not the hospitals, decide which brands will be used and which devices will be selected from each brand. Cultural norms dictate that surgeons comply with the recommendations of the medical group, proposing modifications to the device formulary if needed but not unilaterally using devices from outside the contracted brands and models.

St. Jude Medical Center participates in the technology assessment committee for St. Joseph Health, benefiting from the

TABLE 3

Structure of device assessment and purchasing

	St. Jude Medical Center	Fountain Valley Regional Hospital	Hoag Orthopedic Institute	Long Beach Memorial Medical Center	Kaiser Permanente Irvine Medical Center
Device assessment framework	System-wide committee with physician participation	Emphasis on physician autonomy	Physician and hospital committee	Facility-level committees with weak physician participation	System-wide physician-led committees for each specialty
Physician contract compliance	Moderate	Variable	Strong	Weak	Strong
Experiences with reducing number of vendors	Major focus of strategy; difficult to coordinate among facilities	No interference with physician preferences	Reduced from 3 to 2; significant price reductions achieved	No interference with physician preferences	Reduced from 3 to 2; significant price reductions achieved
Number of vendors (orthopedics)	3	4	2	8	2

Problems with "upselling" by vendors	Yes	Declining	Limited	Yes	Limited
Response to physician conflicts of interest	Disclosure mandated for physicians on technology committees	No mandated disclosure or limits	Mandated disclosure for all physicians	Mandate for disclosure but only weakly enforced	Full ban on financial relations with vendors
Relations with device firms	Contentious but improving	Contentious but good for cardiac	Contentious but improving	Contentious and not improving	Good relations due to large market share
Duration of contracts (years)	3	2	2	1–2	5

scale offered by a multihospital system. In contrast with Kaiser, however, the committees at St. Joseph Health have a stronger management role. It has been difficult to enforce compliance across the hospitals whose physicians remain independent of one another, but the formation of a system-wide clinical effectiveness committee in 2010, with physician members from each facility, has improved coordination and cooperation. For their part, Fountain Valley and Long Beach Memorial belong to hospital systems that have technology assessment committees on paper but where physician participation and compliance has been limited.

The five hospitals differ in their desire and ability to channel technology purchases to a limited number of suppliers. Eight firms dominate the market for orthopedic implants in the United States, but their product lines overlap considerably. Even the largest hospitals do not need more than two or perhaps three firms to support their surgeons' needs. Kaiser Permanente historically contracted with three of the eight manufacturers. Recently it dropped one firm and obtained major price and service concessions from the remaining two. However, its preference would be to contract with three or four suppliers, so as to have immediate access to all newly developed product models. Hoag hospital historically offered the full range of vendors to its physicians, but after the formation of the joint venture it focused its purchases on three suppliers and, eventually, on just two.

The surgeons at St. Jude Medical Center use only two orthopedic firms, but the physicians at other St. Joseph Health facilities have not accepted those choices. The system as whole maintains contracts with three suppliers and would prefer to narrow down to two. Fountain Valley and Long Beach Memorial are not able to reduce the number of suppliers due to an inability to limit physician financial ties with device representatives. At the time of the study, Long Beach Memorial contracted with all eight orthopedic firms, whereas Fountain Valley contracted with the four suppliers desired by its surgeons.

The hospitals have historically had major problems with the upselling to surgeons of expensive devices by manufacturers and distributors. All five have sought to limit physician conflicts of interest, usually beginning with disclosure of financial ties. St. Jude and Hoag require disclosure from physicians participating in technology assessment and purchasing functions, but not from other practicing physicians. Neither Fountain Valley nor Long Beach Memorial is able to enforce financial disclosures. In contrast, Kaiser Permanente bans all financial relationships between physicians and suppliers.

Despite talk of partnership between the buyers and sellers of medical devices, few hospitals and manufacturers have achieved a collaborative relationship. St. Jude and Hoag have been able to develop mutually respectful relationships with suppliers after the contentious restriction in the number of contracts. Vendor relationships at Fountain Valley and Long Beach Memorial remain difficult, with hospitals and manufacturers vying for physician loyalty and short-term negotiating advantages. Kaiser Permanente enjoys the best supplier relationships due to its sophisticated technology assessment, physician leadership, large purchasing volume, and credible threat to terminate unsatisfactory contracts. The nature of the relationships is evidenced in the length of the contract terms. Fountain Valley, Hoag, and Long Beach negotiate two-year contracts. St. Jude is willing to commit to three-year contracts, while Kaiser's contracts cover five years.

PRICING STRATEGY AND OUTCOMES

The five hospitals differ in the prices they pay for medical devices, including established products and newly introduced models. Table 4 summarizes the variability. St. Jude and Fountain Valley assign devices and device components to a product matrix and establish a cap on acceptable prices for each matrix cell. They then extend contracts to all vendors that offer prices below the caps. More recently, St. Jude has sought to limit the number of vendors, regardless of how many offer prices below the matrix cap. Long Beach Memorial experimented with the price cap approach but found manufacturers to substitute low-functionality devices within each matrix cell. At one point almost 90 percent of orthopedic devices had been defined by the vendors as novel and hence as falling outside the matrix. Ultimately the hospital decided to abandon the product matrix and negotiate prices with each vendor individually. Hoag canceled all contracts in 2010 and established a price cap as a percentage of the payment received from insurers. This strategy brought device prices down from 40 percent to 28 percent of insurance reimbursement.

Kaiser requests a first round of price bids from device suppliers and then establishes a price cap based on the observed range. It excludes suppliers that will not price below the cap and then reduces further the number of contractors based on a second round of bids. Kaiser sometimes rotates suppliers to retain attractive prices, but it prefers long contract terms to support mutual investment by the hospital and the device manufacturer in staff training and facility planning. It uses national consulting firms and the Veterans Administration hospitals for pricing benchmarks. The Kaiser health insurance plan accounts for

TABLE 4

Device pricing strategy and outcomes

	St. Jude Medical Center	Fountain Valley Regional Hospital	Hoag Orthopedic Institute	Long Beach Memorial Medical Center	Kaiser Permanente Irvine Medical Center
Pricing strategy for devices	Price matrix, with cap	Unsuccessful use of price matrix; moving to line item pricing	Price cap as a percentage of insurance reimbursement	Price matrix, with negotiated prices	Price matrix, with negotiated prices
Pricing structure for new technology	No price increase without evidence of superiority	New devices paid based on list price	Spine implants paid based on list price	New devices paid based on list price	No price increase without evidence of superiority
Average level of negotiated prices	Moderate	High	Moderate	Moderate	Low
Device price as percentage of Medicare reimbursement	32	43	65	29	Not available

(continued)

TABLE 4
(continued)

	St. Jude Medical Center	Fountain Valley Regional Hospital	Hoag Orthopedic Institute	Long Beach Memorial Medical Center	Kaiser Permanente Irvine Medical Center
Device prices as percentage of private insurer reimbursement	19	42	Declined from 40 to 28	33	Not available
Price variation across hospital chain (orthopedics)	4.8 to 1	2.7 to 1	2.5 to 1	2.8 to 1	No variation

approximately 3 percent of the national market for implantable devices, which gives it substantial pricing leverage. Kaiser maintains a joint registry with utilization and performance data that are useful for price negotiations as well as quality initiatives.

The ability of hospitals to obtain attractive prices depends on the willingness of the surgeons to use contracted devices. Physicians employed by hospital-affiliated medical groups, such as Kaiser Permanente, are socialized to cooperate with the system's device strategies. Contract compliance is high at St. Jude but weaker at St. Joseph Health facilities that lack an employed medical staff. Contract compliance is strong at Hoag due to the ownership alignment with the surgeons. Compliance is variable across the orthopedic, spine, and cardiac service lines at Fountain Valley and Long Beach Memorial, depending on physician personalities and consulting relationships with manufacturers.

Even the most sophisticated product matrix strategy can be undermined if a hospital is obliged to reimburse new products at the manufacturer's list price. St. Jude and Hoag negotiate contract clauses specifying that new devices will be reimbursed at the same level as those they replace unless superior performance is documented to the hospital's technology assessment committee. Long Beach Memorial and Fountain Valley seek to refuse payment for off-contract devices, but their technology assessment committees are not closely aligned with the hospitals' purchasing processes.

SERVICE LINE EFFICIENCY

The course of patient care in a hospital often resembles continuous flow production in manufacturing industries, where major process improvements can be obtained through increased through-put, reduction of waste, lower-cost inputs, performance monitoring, and experience-based modifications. But hospitals traditionally functioned more like artisanal than industrial systems, allowing each physician to practice in his or her idiosyncratic style and neglecting to standardize processes or monitor outcomes in a systematic fashion. This is now changing. Hospitals are beginning to manage technology-intensive service lines using principles of lean manufacturing, just-in-time inventory, and continuous quality improvement.

The redesign of a hospital service line is more complex than the redesign of its supply chain, and requires a more detailed analysis. Rather than delve into all five case studies, it is more illuminating to follow just Kaiser Permanente and the Hoag Orthopedic Institute.[2]

Redesign of Clinical Processes

The joint venture between Hoag hospital and its surgeons embodies the principle that quality and efficiency could best be improved by focusing on a limited range of procedures, thereby reducing the complexity that impedes performance when attempting to offer all services to all patients. A primary objective is to increase the number of procedures that can be done per surgeon, per operating room, and per day. The operating rooms handle five joint replacement procedures per day, a benchmark for the industry. Hoag surgeons work closely with device manufacturers on new products and procedures, and have been pioneers in the development of ambulatory hip replacement surgery. Peripheral orthopedic procedures are performed primarily in ambulatory surgery centers, so as to retain hospital capacity for joint replacement and spine fusion.

The streamlining of care requires the surgeons' acceptance of the facility's clinical standards and processes, relinquishing the individual approaches they used previously. Methods of patient education and preparation for surgery, operating room schedules, procedure timing, staffing, the role of device representatives, protocols for pain medication, laboratory testing, radiology, patient diet, and physical therapy are standardized. This constitutes a major change for the traditionally autonomous orthopedic surgeons. Hoag employs nonsurgical physicians, physician assistants, and technicians to ensure that the surgeons can focus their time in the operating room. The organization embraces the principle that each type of care should be provided by the least expensive, but still competent, level of clinician and facility.

Hoag takes control of discharge planning from the individual physicians. A nurse "navigator" is assigned to each patient's course of care, from preadmission preparation to postdischarge referral. This simplifies the often-confusing transitions from surgery to subacute care, rehabilitation, skilled nursing, and home care. Commercial insurers as well as Medicare pay Hoag using case rates, giving it strong incentives to reduce the patient's length of stay. The surgeons have been happy to relinquish these time-consuming but poorly reimbursed activities to the hospital.

The motivation for process redesign is different at Kaiser Permanente. Rapid growth in health plan enrollment, combined with obesity-driven increases in the patient demand for joint replacement, had created capacity constraints and concerns for waiting lists. The opening of the Irvine hospital and the recruitment of new surgeons only partly alleviated the stress, and the organization identified surgical wait-time as a potential source of enrollee dissatisfaction.

In 2010 Kaiser contracted with a medical device firm's consulting subsidiary to help restructure its surgical scheduling, operating room preparation, procedure cut-to-close times, and postsurgical patient management. The hospital and its orthopedic staff embraced principles of parallel processing and lean manufacturing.[3] Operating room scrub and circulating nurses, technicians, device firm representatives, and other team members influence the rate at which patients are prepared, procedures are conducted, and the operating room is turned around for the next patient.[4] Each surgeon develops his or her team to promote consistency and reduce the need to relearn routine processes. Teams include the anesthesiologist, surgical and circulating nurses, technicians, and device representatives. The medical staff developed the "total joint dance" in recognition of the choreography of postsurgical processes. The two-day length of patient stay is broken down into hourly segments, and the exact timing for antibiotics, pain medications, physical therapy, patient mobilization, and other interventions is specified.

Discharge planning begins prior to admission and continues after surgery. Again, Kaiser sets the industry standard. Permanente physicians are responsible for postsurgical care at rehabilitation and skilled nursing facilities, even though the Kaiser system does not own them. Patients are not discharged from the hospital without a follow-up appointment with both the surgeon and the patient's primary care physician.

Patient Selection and Disease Management

The Hoag Orthopedic Institute and Kaiser Permanente face similar incentives to increase the efficiency of their surgical processes, but different incentives with respect to selecting patients and for managing the underlying disease of osteoarthritis.

After completing the redesign of the operating room and postsurgical recovery, the Kaiser hospital and physicians turned their attention to patient selection and care management for osteoarthritis. Permanente surgeons were spending considerable time assessing patients' disease severity, functional limitations, willingness to lose weight, and attitudes toward surgery. None of these functions is primarily surgical, yet patients were presenting themselves in surgery clinic or were being referred to surgery by primary care physicians without effective triage. Many patients were passive and poorly educated with respect to their treatment options. They used different combinations of analgesic drugs, steroids, and behavioral counseling rather than receiving care based on evidence-based standards.

In 2011 the Kaiser orthopedics department launched the "osteoarthritis care pathway." Clinical pathways are now developed for each type of patient, delineating the roles of surgeons, primary care physicians, nurse practitioners, physical therapists, and wellness coaches. The intent is to the limit the need for surgery through prevention of disease progression, and to limit the involvement of surgeons in nonsurgical processes.

The patient population is segmented by stage of osteoarthritis and by attitudes toward the risks and benefits of surgery. Patients who have failed nonsurgical interventions are triaged into the surgical preparation pathway, with emphasis on education, preoperative weight loss, diabetes management, and planning for postoperative care. Patients without active disease but at risk of eventual surgery are triaged to behavior change programs with wellness coaches. The primary emphasis of the osteoarthritis pathway, however, is on patients at the intermediate stage of disease. These patients are not yet candidates for surgery but need pain management, improved functioning, and prevention of disease progression. Kaiser modified the available clinical guidelines on drug management, radiography, injection of steroids, exercise, weight loss, referral to bariatric surgery, nutritional counseling, and physical therapy and then standardized the process of patient choice among the various pathways.

The Hoag Orthopedic Institute is structured to provide care for patients who seek surgery, not for patients who prefer nonsurgical treatment for their arthritis. It has strong reasons to standardize surgical and postsurgical processes, but no authority to standardize the decision as to which patient is an appropriate candidate for surgery. The decision of whether a particular patient should proceed to surgery reflects the selection criteria used by each surgeon. These criteria are neither standardized by Hoag nor coordinated with the patients' health insurance plan. Patients belong to individual doctors, not to the Hoag Orthopedic Institute. The hospital is paid by insurers on a case rate basis and does not reap any return on investments in chronic care management. Therefore, it does not engage in chronic care management.

The focus of Hoag on orthopedic surgery and postsurgical recovery permits process improvements that could not be implemented by more diversified organizations. This focus leaves Hoag vulnerable, however, to being treated by insurers as a subcontractor at the end of the health care food chain. Upstream organizations can threaten to direct referrals elsewhere if Hoag does not accept ever-lower payment rates. Hoag's efficiency affords it a cost advantage, but it wants to serve as a Center of Excellence for insurers and employers. When its affiliated primary care medical group was acquired by a competitor, the hospital felt impelled to merge with a larger health system to maintain its market position. It selected St. Joseph Health and the Heritage Healthcare medical group. The merger brought Hoag new opportunities as part of the largest hospital system in Orange County, but also the challenge of moving upstream from orthopedic surgery to the management of osteoarthritis.

6

The Patient as Purchaser

The value of a medical technology depends importantly on the choices and actions of the patients who use it, on healthy personal behaviors, shared decision-making with physicians, adherence to evidence-based protocols, self-monitoring, and active participation in recovery and rehabilitation. The patient is a member of the clinical team, and not merely its subject. Increasingly, the patient is also a payer and a purchaser. This chapter begins with the evolution of the patient from a passive recipient of health services to an active participant in the process of care. It then analyzes the structure of consumer cost sharing and the incentives created when different insurance designs are applied to different forms of health care. The chapter concludes with a framework for cost sharing that supports appropriate consumer choice of medical technology.

CONSUMER ENGAGEMENT

Physicians can recommend an intervention but the patient must decide whether to comply and, if so, whether to participate actively or passively. Much attention has been paid in recent years to the failures of adherence to pharmaceutical regimens.[1] Many patients do not fill their prescriptions due to a lack of symptoms, unpleasant side effects, or not remembering when to take what. Failures of adherence are responsible for avoidable complications and the progression of chronic conditions such as diabetes, asthma, and heart disease. The least effective drug is the one never taken.

The value of implantable devices also depends on patient participation. Prior to undergoing major procedures, patients should understand the coming course of treatment, complete all recommended tests, and, for those who are socially minded, connect with patient support groups. Preparation for orthopedic surgery often is referred to as "joint camp" to highlight the importance of building and maintaining muscle strength. Patient engagement after a major procedure includes physical and occupational therapy, adherence to medication and exercise regimens, and appropriate follow-up physician visits. Activation helps reduce pain and discomfort, avoid postsurgical infections and hospital readmissions, and speed the patient's return to normal activities.

Nonfinancial inducements will often outperform financial incentives in encouraging patient engagement. Patients with similar conditions in support groups can share experiences and encourage one another to adopt and sustain health-promoting behaviors. These groups are of particular value for patients receiving complex treatments, such as self-injected specialty drugs for multiple sclerosis, or for patients who face daunting choices, such as medical versus surgical treatment for prostate cancer. Community-based education programs can be adapted to the cultural framework of each patient population, using the language, symbols, and role models most likely to influence behavior.

There is often more than one way to treat a condition, with each option offering a different mix of risks and benefits. It is important that the values and preferences of the patient figure centrally in the choice among alternatives. The contemporary emphasis on shared decision-making is grounded in ethical principles of informed consent and respect for personal autonomy, but it also has important practical consequences for the process and outcome of care. People are more likely to cooperate with the recommendations of their physicians if they participate in the choices made on their behalf. Shared decision-making is particularly important for treatments that are subject to variation in physician recommendations, geographic patterns of care, and patient attitudes toward the treatment alternatives. It is most useful where the patient has the time to discuss the alternatives with family and friends. Some studies suggest that shared decision-making reduces rates of surgery, as informed patients select less invasive treatments, but its primary purpose is to promote engagement. Physicians are skeptical of shared decision-making initiatives that are sponsored by insurers with the principal goal of reducing utilization.[2]

An illustration of the importance of patient preferences can be found in different types of orthopedic surgery, including scheduled knee replacement, repair of traumatic hip fracture, and fusion of spine vertebrae. All these procedures use expensive medical technology, but differ widely in the importance of patient choice for achieving a successful outcome.[3]

There is very little geographic variation in rates of surgery to repair hip fracture. Rates depend on the incidence of falls, automobile collisions, and other forms of trauma, which do not vary widely across regions. There is no debate among physicians as to appropriate treatment, with a strong consensus favoring surgery, and hence only a limited role for shared decision-making. Outcomes are better for patients who adhere to their medications, exercise regimens, and follow-up visits, but hip fracture repair well exemplifies medical procedures that need only modest participation by the patient.

Surgical replacement of arthritic knees exhibits a quite different profile.[4] There is wide geographic variation in rates of surgery. These nonemergency procedures occur in response to increasing pain, but typically can be scheduled and prepared in advance. They allow, and demand, a greater role for patient participation. The progression of arthritic illness can often be slowed, and the need for surgery can be delayed or avoided, if the patient commits to weight loss, exercise, physical therapy, and medication adherence. Knee pain commonly afflicts middle-aged adults who lead active lives, many of whom will seek out medical interventions that permit them to continue doing so. Others are more cautious about the inherent risks of surgery. Patient preferences play a major role in deciding whether the procedure will take place.

Orthopedic surgery professional societies have developed clinical guidelines for knee and hip replacement that recommend surgery only when alternatives have been exhausted.[5] Presurgical interventions include weight loss, exercise, activity modification, or use of walking aids. One study, for example, found that three-quarters of patients participating in water exercise experienced improved function and reduced paid. Pain relief and anti-inflammatory medications reduce and improve function for patients who are unable to successfully manage their condition through behavior modification. Joint damage should be confirmed by imaging prior to surgery, even when patients report severe symptoms. Most patients who undergo joint replacement are very satisfied with the result, but there are concerns for the increasing prevalence of the procedure for younger adults. These patients are at greater risk for implant failure and revision surgery, both because they put greater pressure on the implants and because they live longer with the implants than do older patients. Revision surgery is riskier and has poorer outcomes than primary joint replacement. Younger patients often are less satisfied with their procedures because their expectations are unrealistic. They expect full recovery of function and ability to participate in sports, whereas joint replacement usually permits partial recovery of function and the ability to walk. The wide variation in rates of surgery suggests that joint replacement is characterized by both overtreatment and undertreatment, highlighting the importance of shared decision-making.[6]

Surgical fusion in response to herniated disks or anatomical deformities is beset by even more clinical uncertainty than joint replacement and is even more strongly influenced by patient perceptions and choices. Treatment alternatives include lifestyle changes, pain relief and anti-inflammatory drugs, steroid injections, electrical nerve stimulation, and several types of surgery. The scientific literature is unclear as to which treatment produces the best outcomes, and patients vary widely in their hopes, fears, and willingness to participate actively in their own care. The major comparison of surgical versus nonsurgical treatment of disk herniation, stenosis, and other spine abnormalities found small but statistically significant benefits of surgery, though symptoms and functional ability improved almost as much for patients obtaining nonsurgical care.[7] The comparisons were confounded by the strong role of patient preferences. Only half the patients assigned to surgical treatment went forward with the procedure, while 30 percent of patients assigned to nonsurgical alternatives insisted on receiving surgery.[8]

Shared decision-making recognizes the role of the patient as a decision-maker and not merely the object of decisions made by others.[9] It promotes conversations between patients and physicians covering alternative treatments, relative risks and benefits, and the patient's attitudes toward pain, functionality, and longevity. This process is supported by decision and communication aids, such as print, online, and interactive video materials, that combine clinical evidence with the experiences of patients who have selected each option. Decision aids improve patient understanding and satisfaction with care, the quality of the physician-patient interaction, and, in some cases, the outcome of the treatment chosen.[10] Educational materials can be supported by structured interactions with health coaches who help the patient understand the materials, develop lists of questions for the physician, and ensure that appointments are recorded and followed up with postvisit summaries.[11]

CONSUMER COST SHARING

Consumers should help pay for their care, but the current structure of cost sharing often undermines rather than supports choice. We need to think clearly about the goals of cost sharing and then structure insurance benefits to achieve them.

The first goal of insurance design is to support consumer demand for effective forms of care and discourage use of ineffective treatments. Patients sometimes seek aggressive intervention for symptoms that physicians know are not serious or amenable to treatment. American popular culture is a fertile ground for imaginary illnesses and unrealistic expectations, in part due to sophisticated direct-to-consumer advertising by drug, device, and diagnostics firms. Many minor conditions resolve themselves without professional intervention, and many serious conditions cannot be cured but can only be endured. Yet patients often demand access to technologies whose health benefits are negligible and whose economic costs are significant, knowing their insurance will pay the bill. The overuse of ineffective medical technologies is accompanied by the underuse of effective ones. Consumer cost sharing has been found to reduce patient demand for valuable preventive screenings, drugs, and laboratory tests.[12] Failures of adherence are common for patients with high blood pressure, elevated cholesterol, and other chronic conditions. Some patients with disabling arthritis refuse joint replacement. Even patients suffering from severe illnesses such as lung cancer sometimes discontinue prescribed medications because they experience unpleasant side effects or do not understand the progression of the underlying disease. These causes of underuse are aggravated by insurance designs that require the consumer to pay part of the cost of the care.

The second goal of cost sharing is to encourage patients to favor cheaper over more expensive treatments when they are therapeutically equivalent. Similar health care products are often priced at very different levels. This variance is not surprising when one considers the incentives faced by providers and producers. Competition centers on patient convenience and amenities, rather than price, since most patients are well insured and not expected the pay the difference between the high-priced and the low-priced alternatives. This lack of price-sensitivity undermines the normal market incentive for manufacturers to develop products that are cheaper as well as better than those they replace. The insurer should not pay more for one product if an equally effective alternative is available. The patient, not the insurer, should pay the extra cost of selecting the more expensive variant.

COST-SHARING INSTRUMENTS

There are several ways to require consumers to share in the cost of the services they use. Each form of cost sharing impacts some forms of health care more than others, and so insurance designs combine several instruments and modify the mix over time.

The economically most important cost-sharing instrument is the annual deductible, which requires patients to pay all the costs of care incurred during the year until a defined dollar limit is reached, after which the insurer assumes responsibility. Deductibles reduce the administrative burden of adjudicating small insurance claims and give consumers the incentive to think twice before rushing to the physician's office for minor injuries and illnesses. Deductibles also stimulate comparison-shopping, since the patient rather than the insurer pays the higher fees demanded by more expensive providers. In recent years many employers and insurers have adopted "high-deductible health plans" that require thousands of dollars in out-of-pocket payments.[13] These high-deductible plans sometimes are paired with tax-exempt health care savings accounts. The combination of high deductibles and tax-favored accounts changes the patient's choice structure from "use it or lose it" to "use it or save it," since funds not spent on one service are retained by the patient and spent later on another service, rather than reverting to the insurer.

Deductibles suffer from several important limitations. Most obviously, they do not differentiate between effective and ineffective services. Deductibles implicitly assume that costs incurred below the annual limit are discretionary and should be the responsibility of the patient, while costs incurred above the limit are nondiscretionary and should be the responsibility of the insurer. Deductibles are reset at the start of each calendar year, and so a treatment is more likely to be reimbursed in January than in December. Deductibles create an excessive deterrent for low-cost primary care services but an insufficient deterrent for high-cost specialty services. For example, patients with arthritis who are subject to a deductible must pay for counseling, nutrition, weight loss, and medications out of their own pockets, but shift to the insurer most of the cost of surgical joint replacement. And once they have decided to pursue surgery, patients have no incentive to compare the prices charged by different hospitals, since all the prices fall above the deductible limit. Is this the pattern of incentives we wish to create?

Consumer incentives to compare price with performance can be extended beyond the deductible by adding coinsurance. Under coinsurance, the patient is responsible for paying part of the cost of the services used, with the insurer covering the remainder. Coinsurance is usually subject to an annual out-of-pocket maximum, which protects the consumer from the financial risks of catastrophic illness. The reach of coinsurance can extend far above a deductible limit. A 20 percent coinsurance requirement with a $5000 out-of-pocket maximum, for example, keeps the patient contributing until $25,000 in total treatment costs has been incurred. As such, it influences choices among much more expensive services than would be the case with a deductible.

Coinsurance brings many surgical procedures, imaging tests, and specialty drugs into the patient's shared financial responsibility. It exposes the patient to part of the difference in prices charged by competing providers, in turn encouraging those providers to discount their fees. A major challenge facing coinsurance is that consumers typically do not know their financial exposure in advance of selecting a product or provider. Even if the price of each individual service were available, there would be no way of knowing how many different tests, procedures, and follow-up visits would eventually be needed. Coinsurance makes the patient responsible for a defined percentage of an undefined number. Consumers also need information on the quality of care offered by competing providers and products. Remarkably, price information has been as difficult to obtain in health care as information on quality.

Fixed dollar copayments specify the patient's financial responsibility for each test and treatment without regard to its ultimate price. For example, the patient may be required to pay $20 for a physician office visit and $250 for a procedure in an ambulatory surgery facility, regardless of the price negotiated by the insurer. Products charging different prices can be assigned by the insurer to different benefit tiers, with higher consumer copayments required for those in higher-priced tiers. Rather than being aware of the price of each specific product, the consumer just needs to know which benefit tier it falls into. Most employers and insurers use this tiered structure for their pharmaceutical formularies, requiring a low copayment for cheap generic drugs, a moderate copayment for discounted brand drugs, and a high copayment for nondiscounted brands. Some add a fourth tier for specialty drugs, requiring percentage coinsurance.[14] For example, a drug formulary could require $10 for a generic, $25 for a discounted brand, $50 for a nondiscounted brand, and 25 percent for a specialty drug. Tiered formularies have significantly reduced drug expenditures by inducing consumers to switch from branded to generic drugs and by inducing manufacturers to discount the prices of their branded products.[15]

Under reference pricing, the patient is allowed to select any product or provider, regardless of the price charged. However, the insurer sets a limit to how much it will contribute toward covering the cost. The contribution is set at a level adequate to cover the price charged by efficient products or providers, but below the prices charged by the expensive variants. The consumer is required to pay the difference between the insurer's contribution and the actual price charged. Reference pricing may be thought of as a "reverse deductible." Rather than the patient paying the price up to a defined limit and the insurer covering the remainder, the insurer pays up to a defined limit and the patient pays the remainder. This exposes the patient to the variation in prices for treatments that fall above the deductible. It contrasts with copayment designs, in which the consumer pays a fixed amount regardless of the price actually charged, and with coinsurance designs, in which the consumer pays only a percentage of the difference. The patient's contribution is not limited by an annual out-of-pocket maximum since the insurer has set the reference price at a level that fully covers half of the options.

The services that lend themselves best to reference pricing exhibit considerable variability in prices but little variability in quality. If there are no significant price differences, there is no reason for the insurer to set a contribution threshold. And if there are significant quality differences, reference pricing could potentially channel patients to low-quality providers. Many forms of medical technology fit the criteria for reference pricing. Drugs are highly standardized and the quality of diagnostic tests does not vary widely across laboratories. The predictive value of imaging modalities does not depend on whether the tests were administered in a hospital outpatient department, an ambulatory clinic, or a physician's office. Yet the prices of these services often vary fivefold even within the same local market.

VALUE-BASED INSURANCE DESIGN

Insurance was originally created to protect patients from the financial costs of severe illness, not as a means of guiding consumer choices among treatment options. The most expensive services received the most comprehensive coverage, regardless of their effectiveness. Hospital admissions were covered better than physician visits, specialty procedures better than primary care, and expensive technologies better than cheaper alternatives. Over time, however, employers and governmental programs expanded coverage and reduced cost sharing. During the past thirty years coverage has been extended to preventive care, mental health, outpatient pharmaceuticals, and a host of ancillary products and services. Deductibles and coinsurance declined in importance during most of this period.[16]

An unfortunate side effect of the decline in consumer cost sharing was the increased use of inappropriate and overpriced services. Comprehensive benefits fostered a sense of entitlement among consumers, making it harder for employers, insurers, and government initiatives to address health care costs. Over time, however, continued inflation dampened enthusiasm among purchasers for comprehensive insurance benefits, and renewed their appreciation of cost sharing.[17] Around 2000 the trends in benefit design reversed. The typical deductible increased from several hundred towards several thousand dollars per year. Percentage coinsurance was substituted for dollar copayments. Employees and retirees were expected to pay a larger share of the insurance premium, giving them the incentive to pick plan designs with thinner benefit coverage but lower cost.

Now consumer demand has lurched from overuse to underuse of many services. Patients suffering from chronic illnesses often neglect routine monitoring and medications. Patients facing coinsurance for diagnostic tests, biopharmaceuticals, and surgical procedures often go into debt or refuse the treatment altogether. Fortunately, the worst is being avoided. The contemporary trend in insurance design combines an increase in cost-sharing requirements with a greater readiness to waive the requirements for particularly effective services. If pursued consistently, the dual approach of raising overall cost sharing while waiving it for effective services can improve the incentives facing consumers. We need to be clear on the principles. Insurance should be designed to improve consumer choices, not to protect financial assets. Coverage should not be generous for costly services and skimpy for cheap alternatives. Rather, it should be generous for effective services and skimpy for ineffective alternatives. This framework is quite different from the one that emphasizes financial protection. It has been referred to as "value-based insurance design."[18]

Value-based insurance designs have been applied to chronic conditions such as diabetes and heart disease. Several employers and insurers have eliminated copayments for drugs treating these conditions, regardless of their price.[19] Others have eliminated deductible requirements for prenatal care, well-baby visits, and other forms of primary care.[20] Full coverage of preventive services has been mandated for insurance products under provisions of the Affordable Care Act.[21] Value-based insurance design has not yet been applied to high-cost specialty technologies and procedures. Its principles are broadly applicable, however, and can provide guidance on how to structure cost sharing to support effective purchasing and use.[22] It can be used to structure incentives both for patient engagement and for price shopping.

INCENTIVES FOR PATIENT ENGAGEMENT

Education is the principal instrument by which society should encourage patients to engage in their own health care and improve the effectiveness of medical technology. Financial incentives should play only a secondary role, since patients are often worried, confused, and in a poor position to make rational decisions. Financial incentives are more effectively focused on providers rather than patients, such as by paying higher rates to physicians who incorporate shared decision-making and active disease management into their practices.

But while education should play the primary role, economic incentives can also encourage patient engagement. Insurance inevitably influences choices, and should be designed to encourage good choices and discourage bad ones. Patients should be rewarded for making healthy lifestyle changes, sharing in decisions with their physicians, adhering to the chosen course of care, and, more generally, doing what they can to improve outcomes. They should not be rewarded for using unnecessary treatments or for favoring high-cost products over cheaper and equally effective alternatives.

In principle, financial incentives to promote patient engagement could be offered in the form of payments from the insurer to the patient. But it is difficult to structure positive incentives without requiring the insurer to pay for behaviors that some patients would engage in anyway, in turn increasing premium expenses. As a practical matter, it is usually easier to offer indirect incentives. And as a cultural matter, it is easier to say no and then yes, requiring cost sharing and then waiving it if the patient makes good choices, than it is to say yes and then no, offering comprehensive coverage and then imposing cost sharing on ineffective services.

Medication adherence is essential for slowing the progression of chronic conditions such as asthma and diabetes. The first application of value-based insurance principles was to drugs that treat these conditions. But good outcomes also require patients to make changes in their lifestyle. These changes are difficult. Many patients who start with the best of intentions fall back into poor habits over time. Disease management programs, especially those recommended by trusted sources such as the patient's personal physician, provide support and reminders that help patients stay on the desired path. Participation could and should be encouraged by reducing the patient's deductible, waiving copayments for particular services, or contributing supplemental funds to the patient's health savings account.

Active engagement is even more important for patients suffering from cancer and other conditions treated by expensive specialty pharmaceuticals. Patients need to come regularly to the physician's office or hospital clinic for assessment, review of the treatment protocol, counseling, and infusion of chemotherapies and biologics. Some new specialty drugs can be self-administered by patients, but successful outcomes still require continual monitoring and adjustment of the treatment protocol. The best outcomes are obtained in physician practices that function as "medical homes" for their patients, keeping the office open in the evenings and on the weekends, maintaining registries to track symptoms and treatments, employing social workers to help patients understand their illness and comply with their treatment, and, more generally, pursuing a proactive rather than reactive approach to patient care. Consumers could and should be encouraged to affiliate with medical homes that offer these valuable services.

Patients scheduled for surgery can improve the likelihood of a good outcome if they are educated beforehand as to what to expect, comply with the prescribed tests before the procedure, take seriously the need for exercise and physical therapy after the procedure, and remain engaged after discharge. Some insurers and hospitals offer programs that assist the patient in these activities, and patients should be rewarded for their participation. Hospitalization copayments could be waived for patients who participate in presurgical programs. Cost sharing could be eliminated for postsurgical physical therapy and rehabilitation. Patients who use designated Centers of Excellence could face less cost sharing than patients who insist on using hospitals that lack a commensurate commitment to quality.

INCENTIVES FOR PRICE SHOPPING

Some drugs and devices have only one brand, but most are developed and marketed by more than one firm. Insurance should reward consumer choice of cheaper options unless the more expensive variants can document better outcomes. There is no reason to pay more than the price of the least costly alternative. A shift in consumer incentives from passive to active shopper would strengthen the incentive for producers to develop more efficient products. Without consumer cost sharing, producers will compete based on convenience, extra functionality, and other amenities rather than price. Products will become ever more attractive and ever less affordable. This well describes our contemporary health care system.

Consumers should not face cost sharing for medical technologies that lack effective alternatives. Consumers lack any ability to economize. Where they have choices, however, consumers should face reference pricing, coinsurance, or copayment incentives to select the least costly alternative. Unfortunately, many contemporary insurance designs give quite different incentives. They impose high cost sharing on breakthrough technologies that are expensive, despite the fact that the patient has no alternatives, while extending generous coverage to products that face alternatives and should be competing based on price. A few examples illustrate the paradox.

Pharmaceutical firms have created numerous products to treat osteoarthritis, high blood pressure, and other prevalent conditions in the anticipation that large volumes will create large profits. These blockbuster drugs differ slightly from one another in chemical structure and mechanism of action, but typically create clinically similar benefits. Physicians can switch patients from one drug to another without adverse effect. Insurers have developed tiered formularies to stimulate price competition in these contexts, with higher copayments required for the more expensive brands. Consumers have changed their behavior in response.[23] Price competition has reduced pressures on employers' budgets, increased patient adherence, and improved health outcomes. Lower prices and increased adher-

ence to statins for heart disease, for example, have been credited
with major reductions in complications and fatalities.[24]

Most drugs for rare "orphan" conditions face no therapeutically equivalent competitors. These rare diseases lack sufficient
patient volume to justify research expenditures for more than
one product. Their monopoly status allows drugs for orphan
conditions to be priced at hundreds of thousands of dollars per
year. Unfortunately, many patients face coinsurance and must
rely on financial contributions from pharmaceutical manufacturers, charitable foundations, and family members. According
to the principles of value-based insurance design, patients needing these drugs should be exempted from cost sharing. If and
when multiple treatments are developed for rare conditions,
however, cost sharing could play a valuable role. Rheumatoid
arthritis, for example, afflicts hundreds of thousands of patients
each year, and hence is far from an orphan condition, but until
recently patients had very few effective treatments. There now
exist more than five effective specialty drugs, however, with
meaningful differences in price. Insurers are relying on medical
management programs to favor brands willing to discount their
prices, but they could supplement these physician incentives
with inducements for patients to concern themselves with
costs.[25]

Similar patterns are observed for implantable medical devices.
Competing orthopedic devices often feature slightly different
designs while offering similar patient benefits. Orthopedics firms
charge quite different prices for their products, depending on
whether the insurer or hospital can deliver a steady volume
of sales. As noted in chapter 4, prices for joint implants vary three-
fold, even after adjusting for patient diagnoses and comorbidities.
Formularies with tiered copayments may be appropriate for some

implantable devices. Manufacturers have traditionally marketed devices to physicians, but have begun to advertise directly to patients. The future trajectory may be seen in the artificial knee implant. All brands come in multiple sizes to accommodate differences in patient size. One manufacturer, however, used minor differences in male and female leg anatomy to justify the development of a gender-specific implant. It priced the female-specific implant at a level significantly higher than what was charged for similarly sized versions of the gender-neutral model, despite the absence of evidence on improved performance.[26] It then sold the device through an intense direct-to-consumer marketing campaign.[27] This type of product development could be countered by reference pricing, with the insurer's contribution pegged to the price of the lower-cost model, with exceptions being made for patients whose physicians could demonstrate need for the more expensive variant.

Preventive screening for cancer is a valuable but often underused medical technology. The focus of financial incentives should be to encourage, not discourage, it widespread use. The Affordable Care Act appropriately prohibited cost sharing for preventive cancer screening tests. But the same test is often priced at quite different levels by different clinics and hospitals. For example, Safeway, a national food retailer, realized it was paying prices for diagnostic colonoscopy that ranged from $700 to $7000 in the same local markets. It established a national reference price of $1,250 for the test and required employees who insisted on using higher-priced providers to pay the remainder with their own money.[28] Reference pricing ensured free access to the test for patients willing to help the employer economize, while requiring patients to pay part of the cost if they selected high-priced providers.

CONCLUSION

When appropriately structured, cost sharing aligns the incentives facing the patient with the interests of society. It embodies the principle that the community is willing to subsidize, but not indiscriminately reimburse, the medical choices made by individual citizens. Consumers cannot expect free access to the best care if they do not do their part. However, if poorly structured, cost sharing can impede access to appropriate services. Patients need to be able to waive out-of-pocket fees if they select and adhere to effective forms of care. Cost sharing should be targeted at inappropriate tests and treatments, not at those that improve health and well-being. It is senseless for society to subsidize medical research and protect intellectual property, require detailed evidence of safety and efficacy as a condition for market access, compare clinical and cost effectiveness, structure provider payments to reward efficient delivery, and then create financial barriers to patient access.

Cost sharing should be required only when the patient, rather than the doctor, is the principal decision-maker. For example, patients with severely compromised heart valves face a choice between surgical and catheter-based valve replacement. The correct choice depends on scientific and clinical matters beyond the understanding of most patients. Incentives for efficiency should rely principally on physician payment methods, not consumer cost sharing. But even in this context, cost sharing can play a role. The FDA seeks to limit complex and expensive heart valve procedures to major hospitals that can document good performance. It is possible, however, that the medical arms race will lead to diffusion of the procedure beyond those centers, as ill-equipped facilities seek a share of the profits and prestige. If this happens, insurers could use cost sharing to channel patients to the high-performing hospitals.

If designed poorly, cost sharing threatens patient access to needed care and weakens manufacturer incentives to invest in research and development. But if designed well, cost sharing improves the value of technology. It encourages consumers to avoid tests and treatments that offer little benefit and to select economical options unless more expensive variants prove their superiority. Cost sharing is consistent with the principle that medical technology is a valuable social resource to be used with care and not an individual entitlement to be abused at will. It will always have a role to play in a patient-centered and consumer-driven health care system.

Implications for the Medical Technology Industry

Value-based purchasing has important implications for the medical technology industry. Established methods of design, manufacturing, marketing, and distribution will not work well in the future. Changes on the demand side of the market force commensurate changes on the supply side. Technology firms will need to find new ways to collaborate with the FDA, insurers, hospitals, physicians, and patients themselves. Developers will supplement premarket assessments with evidence from postmarket surveillance and from studies of comparative clinical effectiveness. They will be able to charge premium prices for breakthrough innovations but will be forced to price competitively for follow-on products and incremental innovations. Manufacturers and distributors will need to work with hospitals and their medical staffs on more efficient methods of inventory, training, and use. They will have to support informed patient choice in the face of higher consumer cost sharing. New products will need to be designed with economic cost as well as clinical benefit in mind. Previous chapters analyzed what purchasers need to do to improve value. This chapter shifts the focus to the producers, and to what they need to do to thrive in the new world of increasingly sophisticated assessment, procurement, pricing, and use of medical technology.

COLLABORATION WITH THE FDA

The life sciences industry has historically viewed the FDA as a necessary but unpleasant hurdle to be overcome by new products seeking access to the market. Drugs have often been submitted for review based on a narrow clinical indication, with the knowledge that many physicians would prescribe them beyond the FDA label to a broader patient population. New device models have often been submitted for FDA clearance as substantially equivalent to existing products in order to avoid the need for supportive clinical data. Once the FDA hurdle was passed, many firms did not continue to fund studies of product performance in clinical trials or under real-world conditions of use.

As the FDA shifts from a focus on prelaunch assessment to include postlaunch surveillance, technology firms will find themselves in relationships with the agency that continue over the entire lifecycle of their product. The FDA will increase its demands for postlaunch studies, especially for drugs approved by accelerated review and for devices approved through PMA supplements or the 510(k) pathway. Firms will need to expand their product's label to new clinical indications rather than rely on off-label use. Manufacturers and independent researchers will analyze performance using insurance claims, electronic patient records, and disease registries. Observational studies fall short of the gold standard of randomized clinical trials, but offer larger sample sizes, longer follow-up periods, and the ability to compare outcomes across multiple indications, settings, and modes of administration. Most importantly, perhaps, postlaunch studies will foster head-to-head product comparisons. Comparative effectiveness research can support physicians needing to choose among treatments for individual patients and insurers seeking to ensure adequate coverage while limiting costs.

Ongoing data collection is essential for supporting the FDA's mission to protect public safety. However, the agency also has the responsibility to reduce regulatory delays so as to foster innovation and support patient access. Patients should not be prohibited from using products that pose risks but that would be safe if administered by experienced providers and targeted at appropriately selected patients. The FDA already has several mechanisms for prioritizing review for breakthrough products. The agency and the industry need to explore additional ways to trade stronger postlaunch surveillance for speedier prelaunch authorization.

Collaboration between the FDA and the life sciences industry will be difficult in the heavily politicized regulatory environment. On one side, the FDA faces critics who interpret any concern for regulatory efficiency as an abrogation of consumer protection. On the other side, the FDA faces pressure from firms seeking to introduce products without thorough assessment. Congress threatens intrusive oversight even as it denies the agency the funding needed for expeditious reviews. The only way forward is through collaborative initiatives that speed new products to market and then keep them there only so long as they have evidence of safety and effectiveness.

COLLABORATION WITH INSURERS

Insurers and innovators share a common interest in having medical technology used on the appropriate patients, according to evidence-based protocols, and in efficient settings. In the short term, however, each is tempted to pursue self-interest at the expense of the other. Insurers claim to have their enrollees' best interests at heart, but retain more of their premium revenues if patients do not use high-cost tests and treatments. Their medical management and payment methods discourage adoption of expensive technologies. For their part, technology firms reap financial benefits from broad use of their products, including those that go beyond the evidence. Marketing efforts too often involve financial inducements that undermine physician professionalism and advertising campaigns that create unrealistic consumer expectations.

The conflicts between producers and payers reflect their positions on opposite sides of the technology market. Manufacturers seek higher revenues, while insurers seek lower costs. Technology firms dedicate themselves to the discovery and development of new products, while insurers seek to ensure the affordability of care. But the conflicts lead to damaging outcomes. Insurers' reluctance to embrace innovation contributes to a negative public image and hostile "patient protection" regulation. Overmarketing tarnishes technology firms and exposes them to "sunshine" mandates, litigation, and price regulation.

The most important area for collaboration between technology firms and health insurers is in coverage policy. New products that demonstrate superiority over existing therapies should obtain full and prompt coverage. But insurers cannot and need not extend coverage to every treatment that achieves FDA approval. In contexts where there exist multiple therapeutically equivalent products, insurers can contract selectively with a few providers to gain price discounts and service enhancements. For their part, technology firms need to accept that comparative effectiveness research will be the foundation for insurance coverage policy. They also need to accept that cost will be included in coverage policy. Insurers in other nations demand evidence of cost effectiveness as part of a coverage application, and it is reasonable that similar evidence be used in the United States.

The search for common ground extends to reimbursement. Payment for new technology should be linked to performance. Insurers must recognize that prices for breakthrough innovations need to be high enough to reward risk-taking and to allow innovators to recoup expenditures on research and development. Pay for performance implies high pay for high performance. But manufacturers will not be able to charge premium prices for follow-on products that offer only incremental improvements in care. Generic drugs, follow-on biologics, and devices that are substantially equivalent to existing products must compete for market share through price discounting, not inappropriate physician inducements and misleading consumer advertising.

Insurers need to limit medical management programs to products and procedures where there is clear evidence of abuse, and to not create administrative delays for physicians prescribing effective treatments. They need to expand the scope of medical management to promote patient adherence. For their part, technology firms must resist the temptation to push the use of their products beyond the FDA label, the scientific literature, and the clinical protocols.

The shared interest in appropriate use extends to methods of provider payment. Insurers should ensure that new payment methods do not penalize effective but expensive treatments. Bundled payments need to be updated regularly to reflect the higher costs associated with newly introduced drugs and devices. Some high-cost technologies may be carved out and reimbursed separately until sufficient experience has accumulated to update payment rates. Some pharmaceutical firms are willing to share the financial risk of new drugs through performance-based contracts. For their part, insurers must accept premium pricing where good outcomes have been documented.

COLLABORATION WITH HOSPITALS

The closer alignment of physicians with hospitals will have dramatic effects on the purchasing of medical technology. Manufacturers must recognize that the integrated delivery system, not the individual physician, is now their principal customer. Conversely, hospitals must not view manufacturers as vendors of undifferentiated commodities that can be purchased in bulk, but as innovators who create the reasons why patients come to the hospital for treatment.

Close physician alignment will foster more sophisticated hospital mechanisms for technology assessment. Leading systems will maintain technology committees whose approval is required for supplies and equipment to be incorporated into patient care. The sales process will move from alcohol-lubricated golf outings to evidence-based committee discussions. For their part, technology firms can support hospital planning by sharing insights into the product pipeline and its implications for patient volumes, staffing, and regulatory compliance.

Hospitals and technology firms are moving toward a new structure of contracting. Hospitals are abandoning the any-willing-vendor strategy they adopted as part of the medical arms race. Selective and multiyear contracting reduces transactions costs, builds trust over time, and supports collaborative investments in care processes. For their part, manufacturers will increasingly assign hospitals to customer tiers based on their sales volume, commitment to long-term relationships, and willingness to streamline product distribution. Technology firms can develop partnerships with top-tier hospitals even as they market their products to all institutions. Hospitals in the top tier will get better prices and better service, while those in lower tiers will face list prices and perfunctory service.

Hospitals and manufacturers share common interests in the reliability of product distribution, given the costs of loss or theft, the damage due to incorrect handling, and the imperative to have the right product in the hands of the physician when the patient is ready for treatment. Some hospitals may substitute their own technicians to support surgeons during routine procedures. Manufacturers should see this as an opportunity to focus their in-house technicians on the most complex procedures. The potential for collaboration extends to inventory management. Both parties want to minimize the risk that innovation will reduce the value of existing stocks of supplies and equipment. Product developers have a comparative advantage over hospitals in understanding technology trends and in ensuring just-in-time delivery.

Once committed to long-term relationships, hospitals can help technology firms improve their product designs. This is especially true for implantable devices, where much innovation is accomplished in the clinical setting. Practicing physicians can generate ideas on how to make devices smaller, stronger, and cheaper, on how to combine devices with drugs to reduce infection and inflammation, and on how to use remote monitoring to obtain performance feedback. The collaborative redesign of surgical service lines can reduce the invasiveness of procedures, reduce complications and readmissions, improve discharge planning, reduce patient length of stay, and allow care to move to outpatient settings. The hospitals' ability to thrive financially depends on the pipeline of new medical technology. Without innovation in medical technology, hospitals are just facilities for palliative care, not centers for advanced diagnosis, treatment, and cure.

COLLABORATION WITH CONSUMERS

The medical technology industry must shift its focus from the product to the patient. The effectiveness of a new test or treatment depends on whether the patient understands the range of possible interventions, shares with the physician in the clinical decision-making, adheres to the chosen course of care, and makes the changes in personal behavior that promote good outcomes. As technology firms are pressured to demonstrate the value of their products under real-world conditions of use, it will be ever more important that they collaborate with consumers.

Technology firms are already committed to programs that improve patient education and engagement. All firms generate print and online materials for patients facing treatment alternatives. Some collaborate with insurers on disease management programs that target self-care and medication adherence. Many help patients navigate the requirements for referral, second opinion, prior authorization, step therapy, and specialty pharmacy distribution. Some sponsor public education programs to highlight the importance of underdiagnosed conditions.

Manufacturers play an important role in ensuring patients' financial access to their products. Many insurance designs impose punitive cost sharing on high-cost treatments, even if they are used in accord with evidence-based clinical protocols. And millions of consumers have no health insurance at all. Many manufacturers finance programs that cover the copayments required of insured patients and offer free products to those who are uninsured. Much of the support is channeled through charitable foundations that support consumers regardless of which drug, device, or diagnostic test is selected. These subsidy programs remediate one of the most serious ethical lapses in the health care system, the imposition of heavy cost-sharing burdens on those least able to pay.

The advantages to technology manufacturers of programs that combat underuse are obvious. Programs that combat overuse offer less obvious benefits. In the long term, however, the success of the technology industry depends on how it is perceived by policymakers, the medical profession, and the public. Aggressive sales tactics have already cost the industry incalculable sums. Inappropriate "buy-and-bill" drug markups, consulting honoraria, ghostwritten journal articles, biased medical education programs, misleading direct-to-consumer advertising, and other forms of inducement foster a climate in which the industry is part of the problem rather than part of the solution. No wonder it endures ever more mandates and prohibitions.

THE DESIGN OF INNOVATION

Innovation is stimulated by scientific progress and the application of insights from the entire knowledge-based economy. But successful innovation also requires attention to the needs, preferences, and budgets of purchasers and consumers. In most sectors of the economy, innovators develop products with features aligned to what the consumer wants and is willing to pay for.

Products that cost more than the value placed on them by users do not find users. Firms that miss changes in consumer preferences lose market share and eventually disappear. As we look into the future of medical technology, there is much to be learned from how other sectors have responded to consumer values and valuations.

At risk of oversimplification, firms face two classes of customers. Their most-appreciated buyers are willing to pay top prices and favor continued improvement in product performance and functionality. These are the most loyal and profitable patrons, the ones to whom firms listen most carefully. The less-appreciated customers have more modest budgets and a weaker interest in product functionality. These shoppers are less loyal and more willing to switch to lower-priced competitors. Some are not actual customers at all, since the firm's prices are already out of their reach.

Some firms can focus on high-margin buyers and leave the fickle and budget-minded customers to someone else. Luxury brands and concierge services will always find willing patrons. But for most products and services, the number of low-margin, modest-budget customers is large and can be ignored only at peril. These buyers constitute an initial customer base for new firms that are willing to enter the market with "good-enough" products, establish a presence, and then move up into once-loyal customer segments. This process of disruptive innovation has been observed in numerous markets, from automobiles and computers to hotels and investment banking.

The market for medical technology is ready for disruptive innovation. For decades, life sciences firms responded to cost-unconscious demand by developing high-performance, high-cost products. The FDA was concerned exclusively with safety and efficacy. Insurers extended coverage to new technologies even if they charged prices higher than existing treatments. Physicians always wanted new tests and treatments for their patients, regardless of cost. Hospitals knew their most profitable services were those that employed the most expensive facilities, supplies, and equipment. Well-insured patients thought of health care as an individual right rather than a scarce social resource.

Research-based innovators will pursue breakthroughs that can be priced at premium levels. Purchasers are willing to pay more to get more. The biggest market for medical technology in coming years, however, will consist of cost-effective products that fit within constrained budgets. Some of these products will originate in the developing world, where populations are large but parsimony is imperative. Today's examples include generic drugs, follow-on biologics, plain-vanilla implantable devices, self-administered lab tests, and simplified imaging equipment. Tomorrow's products will span the entire range of medical technology.

CONCLUSION

Innovation is a bond between the present and the future, a transfer of resources from today's society that finances research to tomorrow's society that benefits from new treatments. We need to purchase the technology of today with an eye on the technology of tomorrow. For the FDA, this implies lower barriers to initial market access, more extensive postmarket surveillance, and a willingness to retract authorization for products found to be unsafe or ineffective. For insurers, it implies rapid coverage and generous pricing for breakthrough products, thereby allowing evidence to accumulate and products to improve with experience, coupled with price discounting for follow-on therapies and medical management for inappropriate uses. For physicians and hospitals, it implies methods of payment that reward improved product assessment, procurement, and use. For consumers, it implies a structure of cost sharing that encourages adherence to evidence-based care and discourages demand for overpriced services.

The health care system has suffered from a deficit of effective purchasing, but this deficit is being overcome. Purchasing is becoming more sophisticated, cost-conscious, and value-based. The bar for innovation is rising.

NOTES

INTRODUCTION

1. Mary Thompson, "As TAVI Advances, Adjunctive Devices Multiply," *MedTech Insight* (December 2011), reprinted in Mary Thompson, ed., *Heart Valves* (Elsevier Business Intelligence Special Reports: Innovation Series, 2013), pp. 43–53; Bill Berkrot, "Heart Device Approval Delays Leave US Doctors Frustrated," *Reuters*, May 27, 2013; Joanne K. Wuensch, *Sizing Up the TAVR Market and New Technologies* (New York: BMO Capital Markets, June 2013); Stephen Levin, "SYMETIS: Well-Positioned Next-Generation TAVI Player," *In Vivo* (April 2012), reprinted in Thompson, *Heart Valves*, pp. 33–41.

2. Steven M. Kurtz et al., "The Impact of the Economic Downturn on Total Joint Replacement Demand in the United States," *Journal of Bone and Joint Surgery* 96 (2014): 624–630.

1. REGULATORY ACCESS TO THE MARKET

1. Henry G. Grabowski and John M. Vernon, "Effective Patent Life in Pharmaceuticals," *International Journal of Technology Management* 19, no. 1–2 (2000): 98–120.

2. Joseph A. DiMasi et al., "The Price of Innovation: New Estimates of Drug Development Costs," *Journal of Health Economics* 22, no. 2 (March 2003): 151–185.

3. Ernst R. Berndt et al., "Industry Funding of the FDA: Effects of PDUFA on Approval Times and Withdrawal Rates," *Nature Reviews: Drug Discovery* 4 (July 2005): 545–554.

4. Francis Megerlin et al., "Biosimilars and the European Experience: Implications for the United States," *Health Affairs* 32, no. 10 (October 2013): 1803–1810.

5. Genia Long et al., *Recent Average Price Trends for Implantable Medical Devices, 2007–2011* (Washington, DC: Analysis Group, September 2013).

6. William H. Maisel, "Medical Device Regulation: An Introduction for the Practicing Physician," *Annals of Internal Medicine* 140, no. 4 (February 2004): 296–302.

7. James Weinstein et al., "Surgical vs Nonoperative Treatment for Lumbar Disk Herniation: The Spine Patient Outcomes Research Trial (SPORT): A Randomized Trial," *Journal of the American Medical Association* 296, no. 20 (November 2006): 2441–2450.

8. Institute of Medicine, Committee on the Public Health Effectiveness of the FDA 510(k) Clearance Process, *Medical Devices and the Public's Health: The FDA 510(k) Clearance Process at 35 Years* (Washington, DC: National Academies Press, 2011), p. 4.

9. Sanket S. Dhruva et al., "Strength of Study Evidence Examined by the FDA in Premarket Approval of Cardiac Devices," *Journal of the American Medical Association* 302, no. 24 (December 2009): 2679–2685.

10. Marcia G. Crosse, *Medical Devices: Shortcomings in FDA's Premarket Review, Postmarket Surveillance, and Inspections of Device Manufacturing Establishments* (Washington, DC: United States Government Accountability Office, June 2009).

11. Benjamin N. Rome et al., "FDA Approval of Cardiac Implantable Electronic Devices via Original and Supplement Premarket Approval Pathways, 1979–2012," *Journal of the American Medical Association* 311, no. 4 (January 2014): 385–391.

12. Robert G. Hauser and Adrian K. Almquist, "Learning from Our Mistakes? Testing New ICD Technology," *New England Journal of Medicine* 359 (December 2008): 2517–2519; G. Neal Kay and Kenneth A.

Ellenbogen, "An ICD Lead Advisory: A Plea for More Diligence and More Data," *Pacing and Clinical Electrophysiology* 35, no. 6 (June 2012): 648–649.

13. Institute of Medicine, *Medical Devices and the Public's Health,* p. 4.

14. Ibid., p. 108.

15. Ibid., p. 101.

16. David R. Challoner and William W. Vodra, "Medical Devices and Health—Creating a New Regulatory Framework for Moderate-Risk Devices," *New England Journal of Medicine* 365 (September 2011): 977–979; Gregory D. Curfman and Rita F. Redberg, "Medical Devices—Balancing Regulation and Innovation," *New England Journal of Medicine* 365 (September 2011): 975–977.

17. US Department of Health and Human Services, Food and Drug Administration, *Improvements in Device Review: Results of CDRH's Plan of Action for Premarket Review of Devices* (Washington, DC: Food and Drug Administration, November 2012).

18. Ibid.

19. Agency for Healthcare Research and Quality, *HCUP Nationwide Inpatient Sample (NIS)* (2009); Steven M. Kurtz et al. "The Impact of the Economic Downturn on Total Joint Replacement Demand in the United States," *Journal of Bone and Joint Surgery* 96 (2014): 624–630.

20. Deborah Cohen, "Out of Joint: The Story of the ASR," *British Medical Journal* 342 (May 2011): d2905.

21. Brent M. Ardaugh et al., "The 510(k) Ancestry of a Metal-on-Metal Hip Implant," *New England Journal of Medicine* 368 (January 2013): 97–100.

22. Joshua P. Rising et al., "Delays and Difficulties in Assessing Metal-on-Metal Hip Implants," *New England Journal of Medicine* 367 (July 2012): e1, doi: 10.1056/NEJMp1206794.

23. Jonathan D. Rockoff, "When J & J Learned of Implant Problems," *Wall Street Journal,* January 23, 2013.

24. Jef Feeley and David Voreacos, "J & J Said to Weigh $3 Billion Settlement of Its Hip Implant Cases," *Bloomberg News,* August 20, 2013.

25. Barry Meier, "Johnson & Johnson Said to Agree to $4 Billion Settlement over Hip Implant," *New York Times,* November 12, 2013.

26. Institute of Medicine, *Medical Devices and the Public's Health.*

27. Daniel B. Kramer et al., "Regulation of Medical Devices in the United States and European Union," *New England Journal of Medicine* 366 (March 2012): 848–855; J. Y. Chai, "Medical Device Regulation in the United States and European Union: A Comparative Study," *Food and Drug Law Journal* 55, no. 1 (2000): 57–80; Jonas Schreyögg et al., "Balancing Adoption and Affordability of Medical Devices in Europe," *Health Policy* 92, no. 2–3 (October 2009): 218–224.

28. Andrew Pollack, "Medical Treatment, out of Reach," *New York Times,* February 9, 2011.

29. Amitabh Chandra et al., *The Diffusion of New Medical Technology: The Case of Drug-Eluting Stents* (Washington, DC: National Bureau of Economic Research, June 2013).

30. David R. Holmes and Michael J. Mack, "Transcatheter Valve Therapy: A Professional Society Overview from the American College of Cardiology Foundation and the Society of Thoracic Surgeons," *Journal of the American College of Cardiology* 58, no. 4 (July 2011): 445–455.

31. Stephen Levin, "EDWARDS: Transcatheter Valve Leader Proves You Can Go Home Again," in *Heart Valves,* ed. Mary Thompson (Elsevier Business Intelligence Special Reports: Innovation Series, 2013), pp. 56–70.

32. Mary Thompson, "As TAVI Advances, Adjunctive Devices Multiply," *MedTech Insight* (December 2011), reprinted in Thompson, *Heart Valves,* pp. 43–53; Bill Berkrot, "Heart Device Approval Delays Leave US Doctors Frustrated," *Reuters,* May 27, 2013; Joanne K. Wuensch, *Sizing Up the TAVR Market and New Technologies* (New York: BMO Capital Markets, June 2013); Stephen Levin, "SYMETIS: Well-Positioned Next-Generation TAVI Player," *In Vivo* (April 2012). Reprinted in Thompson, *Heart Valves,* pp. 33–41.

33. Mary Stuart, "Percutaneous Mitral Valve Therapy: The Next Decade," *Start Up* (February 2012). Reprinted in Thompson, *Heart Valves,* pp. 8–20.

34. Peter McCulloch, "The EU's System for Regulating Medical Devices," *British Medical Journal* 345 (October 2012): e7126; Deborah Cohen and Matthew Billingsley, "Europeans Are Left to Their Own Devices," *British Medical Journal* 342 (May 2011): d2748.

35. Ibid.

36. Cohen, "Out of Joint," p. d2905.

37. Rachel E. Behrman et al., "Developing the Sentinel System—a National Resource for Evidence Development," *New England Journal of Medicine* 364 (February 2011): 498–499; Melissa A. Robb et al., "The US Food and Drug Administration's Sentinel Initiative: Expanding the Horizons of Medical Product Safety," *Pharmacoepidemiology and Drug Safety* 21, supplement S1 (January 2012): 9–11.

38. Philip E. Johnson et al., "NCCN Oncology Risk Evaluation and Mitigation Strategies White Paper: Recommendations for Stakeholders," *Journal of the National Comprehensive Cancer Network* 8, supplement 7 (September 2010): S7–S27.

39. Ethan A. Halm et al., "Is Volume Related to Outcome in Health Care? A Systematic Review and Methodologic Critique of the Literature," *Annals of Internal Medicine* 137, no. 6 (September 2002): 511–520; Edward L. Hannan et al., "Coronary Angioplasty Volume-Outcome Relationships for Hospitals and Cardiologists," *Journal of the American Medical Association* 277, no. 11 (March 1997): 892–898.

40. Michael J. Mack and David R. Holmes, "Rational Dispersion for the Introduction of Transcatheter Valve Therapy," *Journal of the American Medical Association* 306, no. 19 (November 2011): 2149–2150.

2. INSURANCE COVERAGE AND REIMBURSEMENT

1. Peter J. Neumann et al., "Medicare's National Coverage Decisions for Technologies, 1999–2007," *Health Affairs* 27, no. 6 (November 2008): 1620–1631.

2. MedPAC, *Report to the Congress: Medicare Payment Policy: An Introduction to How Medicare Makes Coverage Decisions* (Washington, DC: US Government Printing Office, March 2003), appendix B.

3. Sean R. Tunis et al., "Improving the Quality and Efficiency of the Medicare Program through Coverage Policy" (Washington, DC: Urban Institute, August 2011).

4. Ibid.

5. Sanket S. Dhruva and Rita F. Redberg, "Variations between Clinical Trial Participants and Medicare Beneficiaries in Evidence

4

Used for Medicare National Coverage Decisions," *Archives of Internal Medicine* 168, no. 2 (January 2008): 136–140.

6. Neumann et al., "Medicare's National Coverage Decisions."

7. Ibid.

8. Susan B. Foote and Robert J. Town, "Implementing Evidence-Based Medicine through Medicare Coverage Decisions," *Health Affairs* 26, no. 6 (November 2007): 1634–1642.

9. Ibid.

10. Susan B. Foote et al., "Resolving the Tug-of-War between Medicare's National and Local Coverage," *Health Affairs* 23, no. 4 (July 2004): 108–123; US General Accounting Office, *Medicare: Divided Authority for Policies on Coverage of Procedures and Devices Results in Inequities*, publication GAO-03-175 (Washington, DC: US Government Accountability Office, 2003), 16.

11. Susan B. Foote et al., "Variation in Medicare's Local Coverage Policies: Content Analysis of Local Medical Review Policies," *American Journal of Managed Care* 11, no. 3 (March 2001): 181–187.

12. Barry M. Straube, "How Changes in the Medicare Coverage Process Have Facilitated the Spread of New Technologies," *Health Affairs* (June 2005): w314–w316, doi:10.1377/hlthaff.w5.314; Sean R. Tunis and Steven D. Pearson, "Coverage Options for Promising Technologies: Medicare's 'Coverage with Evidence Development,'" *Health Affairs* 25, no. 5 (September 2006): 1218–1230.

13. Tunis et al., "Improving the Quality and Efficiency."

14. Pierantonio Russo and Alan Adler, "How Insurers Can Bear the Burden of Proof for New Treatments," *Managed Care* (December 2009); Mark Perman, "Coverage with Evidence Development Allows Early Adoption, Better Evaluation," *Managed Care* (February 2013).

15. Michael Lanthier et al., "An Improved Approach to Measuring Drug Innovation Finds Steady Rates of First-in-Class Pharmaceuticals, 1987–2011," *Health Affairs* 32, no. 8 (August 2013): 1433–1439.

16. Institute of Medicine, *Learning What Works Best: The Nation's Need for Evidence on Comparative Effectiveness in Health Care* (Washington, DC: National Academies Press, 2007).

17. Kavita Patel, "Health Reform's Tortuous Route to the Patient-Centered Outcomes Research Institute," *Health Affairs* 29, no. 10 (October 2010): 1777–1782.

18. Penny Mohr, "Looking at Comparative Effectiveness Research from Medicare's Perspective," *Journal of Managed Care Pharmacy* 18, no. 4 (May 2012): S05–S08.

19. Steven D. Pearson and Peter B. Bach, "How Medicare Could Use Comparative Effectiveness Research in Deciding on New Coverage and Reimbursement," *Health Affairs* 29, no. 10 (October 2010): 1796–1804.

20. Ibid.

21. Milton C. Weinstein and William B. Stason, "Foundations of Cost-Effectiveness Analysis for Health and Medical Practices," *New England Journal of Medicine* 296 (March 1977): 716–721.

22. Robert Steinbrook, "Saying No Isn't NICE—the Travails of Britain's National Institute for Health and Clinical Excellence," *New England Journal of Medicine* 359 (November 2008): 1977–1981; Ruth R. Faden and Kalipso Chalkidou, "Determining the Value of Drugs—the Evolving British Experience," *New England Journal of Medicine* 364 (April 2011): 1289–1291; Karl Claxton et al., "Value Based Pricing for NHS Drugs: An Opportunity Not to Be Missed?" *British Medical Journal* 336 (January 2008): 251.

23. Zosia Kmietowicz, "Government's Fund Is Improving Access to Drugs for Patients with Cancer," *British Medical Journal* 343 (December 2011): d7918.

24. J.D. Chambers et al., "Factors Predicting Medicare National Coverage," *Medical Care* 50 (2012): 249–256.

25. Peter J. Neumann, "Why Don't Americans Use Cost-Effectiveness Analysis?," *American Journal of Managed Care* 10, no. 5 (May 2004): 308–312.

26. Pearson and Bach, "How Medicare Could Use Comparative Effectiveness Research."

27. James C. Robinson and Jill M. Yegian, "Medical Management after Managed Care," *Health Affairs* (May 2004), doi:10.1377/hlthaff. w4.269.

28. Brian Klepper, "Why Medical Management Will Re-Emerge," *Health Care Blog,* August 1, 2012, http://thehealthcareblog.com/blog/2012/08/01/why-medical-management-will-re-emerge/.

29. James C. Robinson, "Hospital Market Concentration, Prices, and Profitability in Orthopedic Surgery and Interventional Cardiology," *American Journal of Managed Care* 17, no. 6 (June 2011): e241–e248.

30. James C. Robinson, "Hospitals Respond to Medicare Payment Shortfalls by Both Shifting Costs and Cutting Them, Based on Market Concentration," *Health Affairs* 30, no. 7 (July 2011): 1265–1271.

31. Direct costs include staffing, supplies, implantable devices, and other services provided to the individual patient, but do not include the costs of administration and charity care. Contribution margins thus are always higher than profits, which measure the difference between total revenues and total costs.

32. Robinson, "Hospital Market Concentration."

33. Michael Porter and Elizabeth O. Teisberg, *Redefining Health Care: Creating Value-Based Competition on Results* (Cambridge, MA: Harvard Business School Press, 2006).

34. James C. Robinson and Kimberly MacPherson, "Payers Test Reference Pricing and Centers of Excellence to Steer Patients to Low-Price and High-Quality Providers," *Health Affairs* 31, no. 9 (September 2012): 2028–2036.

35. Jaimy Lee, "Wal-Mart, Lowes to Offer Employees Leg Up on Knee and Hip Work—at Certain Systems," *Modern Healthcare,* October 8, 2013, www.modernhealthcare.com/article/20131008/NEWS/310089966/wal-mart-lowes-workers-get-a-leg-up-on-knee-work.

36. Elisabeth Rosenthal, "In Need of a New Hip, but Priced out of the U.S.," *New York Times,* August 3, 2013.

3. METHODS OF PAYMENT FOR MEDICAL TECHNOLOGY

1. Paul Gottlober et al., *Medicare Hospital Prospective Payment System: How DRG Rates Are Calculated and Updated,* publication OEI-09–00–00200 (Office of Inspector General, Office of Evaluation and Inspections, Region IX, August 2001).

2. In practice, Medicare's method of paying hospitals is not purely prospective, since the DRG payments reflect some procedures as well as diagnoses and the overall payment can be supplemented by stop-loss payments for expenditures per patient that are exceptionally high.

3. William H. Rogers et al., "Quality of Care before and after Implementation of the DRG-Based Prospective Payment System: A Summary of Effects," *Journal of the American Medical Association* 264, no. 15 (October 1990): 1989–1994; John E. Wennberg et al., "Will Payment Based on Diagnosis-Related Groups Control Hospital Costs?," *New England Journal of Medicine* 311 (August 1984): 295–300.

4. Rogers et al., "Quality of Care Before and After Implementation," 1989–1994.

5. Boston Scientific, *Device Carve-Out Guide: Insurer Contracting for Neuroendovascular Implantables* (Fremont, CA: Boston Scientific Neurovascular Group, 2004).

6. These data are obtained from a study of patients receiving care in sixty-one hospitals in eight states. They reflect the actual prices paid by hospitals, not the list price posted by the manufacturers.

7. James C. Robinson et al., "Variability in Costs Associated with Total Hip and Knee Replacement Implants," *Journal of Bone and Joint Surgery* 94, no. 18 (September 2012): 1693–1698.

8. Stephen F. Jencks et al. "Rehospitalizations among Patients in the Medicare Fee-for-Service Program," *New England Journal of Medicine* 360 (April 2009): 1418–1428.

9. Ivan M. Tomek et al. "A Collaborative of Leading Health Systems Finds Wide Variations in Total Knee Replacement Delivery and Takes Steps to Improve Value," *Health Affairs* 31, no. 6 (June 2012): 1329–1338.

10. Neeraj Sood et al., "Medicare's Bundled Payment Pilot for Acute and Postacute Care: Analysis and Recommendations on Where to Begin," *Health Affairs* 30, no. 9 (September 2011): 1708–1717; J.C. Robinson, "Administered Pricing and Vertical Integration in the Hospital Industry," *Journal of Law and Economics* 39, no. 1 (1996): 357–378.

11. Joseph P. Newhouse and Alan M. Garber, "Geographic Variation in Health Care Spending in the United States: Insights from an Institute of Medicine Report," *Journal of the American Medical Association* 310, no. 12 (September 2013): 1227–1228.

12. Harold D. Miller, "From Volume to Value: Better Ways to Pay for Health Care," *Health Affairs* 28, no. 5 (September-October 2009): 1418–1428.

13. François de Brantes et al., "Building a Bridge from Fragmentation to Accountability—the Prometheus Payment Model," *New England Journal of Medicine* 361 (September 2009): 1033–1036.

14. Mark Wynn, "Global Payment Demonstrations in the Medicare Program," in *Global Fees for Episodes of Care,* ed. Douglas Emery (New York: McGraw-Hill, 1999), pp. 393–405.

15. Christopher Hund and Maulik Joshi, *Early Learnings from the Bundled Payment Acute Care Episode Demonstration Project* (Chicago: Health Research & Education Trust, April 2011).

16. *BPCI Model 2: Retrospective Acute & Post Acute Care Episode,* CMS. gov, innovation.cms.gov/initiatives/BPCI-Model-2/index.html.

17. Christopher Chen and D. Clay Ackerly, "Beyond ACOs and Bundled Payments: Medicare's Shift toward Accountability in Fee-for-Service," *Journal of the American Medical Association* 331, no. 7 (2014): 673–674.

18. James C. Robinson and Kimberly MacPherson, *Aligning Consumer Cost-Sharing with Episode of Care (EOC) Provider Payments* (Oakland, CA: Integrated Healthcare Association Issue Brief, September 2011).

19. Peter S. Hussey et al., "The PROMETHEUS Bundled Payment Experiment: Slow Start Shows Problems in Implementing New Payment Models," *Health Affairs* 30, no. 11 (November 2011): 2116–2124; Tom Williams and James C. Robinson, "Bundled Episode-of-Care Payment for Orthopedic Surgery: The Integrated Healthcare Association Initiative," September 2013, www.iha.org/pdfs_documents/bundled_payment/Bundled-Payment-Orthopedics-Issue-Brief-September-2013.pdf.

20. Harold D. Miller, "From Volume to Value: Better Ways to Pay for Health Care," *Health Affairs* 28, no. 5 (September-October 2009): 1418–1428.

21. Steven M. Lieberman and John M. Bertko, "Building Regulatory and Operational Flexibility into Accountable Care Organizations and 'Shared Savings,'" *Health Affairs* 30, no. 1 (January 2011): 23–31; James C. Robinson, *Accountable Care Organization for PPO Patients: Challenge and Opportunity in California* (Oakland, CA: Integrated Healthcare Association White Paper, 2011).

22. Chuck Shih and Elise Berliner, "Diffusion of New Technology and Payment Policies: Coronary Stents," *Health Affairs* 27, no. 6 (November 2008): 1566–1576.

23. Patrick W. Serruys et al., "Coronary-Artery Stents," *New England Journal of Medicine* 354 (February 2006): 483–495.

24. Alexandra T. Clyde et al., "Experience with Medicare's New Technology Add-On Payment Program," *Health Affairs* 27, no. 6 (November 2008): 1632–1641.

25. Jonas Schreyögg et al., "Methods to Determine Reimbursement Rates for Diagnosis Related Groups (DRG): A Comparison of Nine European Countries," *Health Care Management Science* 9, no. 3 (August 2006): 215–223.

4. THE HOSPITAL AS PURCHASER

1. Harold S. Luft et al., "Hospital Behavior in a Local Market Context," *Medical Care Research and Review* 43, no. 2 (August 1986): 217–251.

2. Mark Pauly and Michael Redisch, "The Not-for-Profit Hospital as a Physicians' Cooperative," *American Economic Review* 63, no. 1 (March 1973): 87–99.

3. Eliot Freidson, *Profession of Medicine: A Study in the Sociology of Applied Knowledge* (Chicago: University of Chicago Press, 1970).

4. Harold S. Luft et al., "The Role of Specialized Clinical Services in Competition among Hospitals," *Inquiry* 23, no. 1 (Spring 1986): 83–94.

5. James C. Robinson et al., "Competition and the Cost of Hospital Care, 1972–82," *Journal of the American Medical Association* 257, no. 23 (June 1987): 3241–3245.

6. Earl S. Ford et al., "Explaining the Decrease in U.S. Deaths from Coronary Disease, 1980–2000," *New England Journal of Medicine* 356 (June 2007): 2388–2398; David M. Cutler, *Your Money or Your Life: Strong Medicine for America's Health Care System* (New York: Oxford University Press, 2005).

7. James C. Robinson et al., "Market and Regulatory Influences on the Availability of Coronary Angioplasty and Bypass Surgery in U.S. Hospitals," *New England Journal of Medicine* 317 (July 1987): 85–90.

8. MedPAC, *Report to the Congress: Medicare Payment Policy* (Washington, DC: US Government Printing Office, March 2012), chap. 3.

9. Advisory Board Company, *The Highly Productive Cardiovascular Enterprise: Imperatives for Operating at Optimal Efficiency to Safeguard Margins* (Washington, DC: Advisory Board Company, 2012); Advisory Board Company, *Future of Orthopedics: Strategic Forecast for a Service Line under Siege* (Washington, DC: Advisory Board Company, 2004).

10. James C. Robinson, "Decline of Hospital Utilization and Cost Inflation under Managed Care in California," *Journal of the American Medical Association* 276, no. 13 (November 1996): 1060–1064; Anil Bamezai et al., "Price Competition and Hospital Cost Growth in the United States, 1989–1994," *Health Economics* 8, no. 3 (May 1999): 233–243.

11. Community hospitals are defined as "all nonfederal, short-term general, and specialty hospitals whose facilities and services are available to the public."

12. American Hospital Association, *Chartbook, Trends Affecting Hospitals and Health Systems*, chapter 2, "Organizational Trends" (updated September 2013), www.aha.org/research/reports/ tw/chartbook/ch2.shtml.

13. Martin Gaynor and Robert Town, *The Impact of Hospital Consolidation—Update* (Princeton, NJ: Synthesis Project, Robert Wood Johnson Foundation, June 2012).

14. Kanu Okike et al., "Accuracy of Conflict-of-Interest Disclosures Reported by Physicians," *New England Journal of Medicine* 361 (October 2009): 1466–1474.

15. Shantanu Agrawal et al., "The Sunshine Act—Effects on Physicians," *New England Journal of Medicine* 368 (May 2013): 2054–2057.

16. Jean M. Mitchell, "Physician Joint Ventures and Self-Referral: An Empirical Perspective," in *Conflicts of Interest in Clinical Practice and Research*, ed. R.G. Spece et al. (New York: Oxford University Press, 1996), pp. 299–317; Bruce J. Hillman et al., "Physicians' Utilization and Charges for Outpatient Diagnostic Imaging in a Medicare Population," *Journal of the American Medical Association* 268, no. 15 (October 1992): 2050–2054.

17. Jennifer O'Sullivan, *Medicare: Physician Self-Referral ("Stark I and II")* (Washington, DC: Congressional Research Service, 2004).

18. Christina Gutowski, et al., "Health Technology Assessment at the University of California, San Francisco," *Journal of Healthcare Man-

agement 56, no. 1 (2011): 1–16; Advisory Board Company, *Navigating the New Era of Technology Assessment—Strategies and Tools for Working with Value Analysis, Capital Budgeting, and Technology Assessment Companies* (Washington, DC: Advisory Board Company, 2010).

19. Ibid.

20. Oliver E. Williamson, *The Economic Institutions of Capitalism* (New York: Free Press, 1985).

21. This discussion of hospital pricing strategies is based on hospital case studies developed as part of the author's research and participation in the value-purchasing initiative of the Integrated Healthcare Association between 2006 and 2012.

22. Kathleen Montgomery and Eugene S. Schneller, "Hospitals' Strategies for Orchestrating Selection of Physician Preference Items, " *Milbank Quarterly* 85, no. 2 (June 2007): 307–335.

5. ORGANIZATIONAL CAPABILITIES FOR TECHNOLOGY PURCHASING

1. Laurie E. Felland et al., *Community Report: Orange County, California* (Washington, DC: Center for Studying Health System Change, August 2011).

2. James C. Robinson, "Case Studies of Orthopedic Surgery in California: The Virtues of Care Coordination versus Specialization," *Health Affairs* 32, no. 5 (May 2013): 921–928.

3. Depuy Healthcare Solutions Group, *Clinic Optimization: A Consulting Service to Improve Patient Satisfaction* (Rayburn, MA: Healthcare Solutions Group, 2012).

4. An interesting case study of orthopedic process improvements at a major Philadelphia hospital is provided in Richard M.J. Bohmer et al., *Managing Orthopaedics at Rittenhouse Medical Center* (Cambridge, MA: Harvard Business School Case 607-152, June 2007; revised March 2010).

6. THE PATIENT AS PURCHASER

1. Lars Osterberg and Terrence Blaschke, "Adherence to Medication," *New England Journal of Medicine* 353 (August 2005): 487–497.

2. Jiwon Youm et al., "The Emerging Case for Shared Decision Making in Orthopaedics," *Journal of Bone and Joint Surgery* 94, no. 20 (October 2012): 1907–1912.

3. James N. Weinstein et al., "Trends and Geographic Variations in Major Surgery for Degenerative Diseases of the Hip, Knee, and Spine," *Health Affairs* (October 2004), doi: 10.1377/hlthaff.var.81; Elliott S. Fisher et al., *Trends and Regional Variation in Hip, Knee, and Shoulder Replacement* (Dartmouth Atlas Surgery Report, Dartmouth Institute for Health Policy and Clinical Practice, April 6, 2010).

4. Ibid.

5. Weiya Zhang et al., "OARSI Recommendations for the Management of Hip and Knee Osteoarthritis," *Osteoarthritis and Cartilage* 16, no. 2 (February 2008): 137–162.

6. Elliott S. Fisher et al., *Trends and Regional Variation in Hip, Knee, and Shoulder Replacement* (Dartmouth Atlas Surgery Report, Dartmouth Institute for Health Policy and Clinical Practice, April 6, 2010).

7. James N. Weinstein et al., "Surgical versus Nonsurgical Therapy for Lumbar Spinal Stenosis," *New England Journal of Medicine* 358 (February 2008): 794–810.

8. James Weinstein et al., "Surgical vs Nonoperative Treatment for Lumbar Disk Herniation: The Spine Patient Outcomes Research Trial (SPORT): A Randomized Trial," *Journal of the American Medical Association* 296, no. 20 (November 2006): 2441–2450.

9. Cathy Charles et al., "Shared Decision-Making in the Medical Encounter: What Does It Mean?," *Social Science and Medicine* 44, no. 5 (March 1997): 681–692; President's Commission for the Study of Ethical Problems in Medicine and Biomedical and Behavioral Research, *Making Health Care Decisions: The Ethical and Legal Implications of Informed Consent in the Patient Practitioner Relationship* (Washington, DC: US Government Printing Office, 1982).

10. Annette M. O'Connor et al., "Decision Aids for People Facing Health Treatment or Screening Decisions," *Cochrane Database Systematic Review* 3 (2009): CD001431; Simon J. Griffin et al., "Effect on Health-Related Outcomes of Interventions to Alter the Interaction between Patients and Practitioners: A Systematic Review of Trials,"

Annals of Family Medicine 2, no. 6 (November–December 2004): 595–608.

11. Kevin J. Bozic et al., "Emerging Ideas: Shared Decision Making in Patients with Osteoarthritis of the Hip and Knee," *Clinical Orthopedic Related Research* 469, no. 7 (July 2011): 2081–2085.

12. Dana P. Goldman et al., "Prescription Drug Cost Sharing: Associations with Medication and Medical Utilization and Spending and Health," *Journal of the American Medical Association* 298, no. 1 (July 2007): 61–69; Joseph P. Newhouse and the Insurance Experiment Group, *Free for All? Lessons from the RAND Health Insurance Experiment* (Cambridge, MA: Harvard University Press, 1994).

13. Gary Claxton et al., *Employer Health Benefits: 2013 Annual Survey* (Menlo Park, CA: Kaiser Family Foundation and Health Research & Education Trust, 2013).

14. Pharmacy Benefit Management Institute, *2013–2014 Prescription Drug Benefit Cost and Plan Design Report* (Plano, TX: Pharmacy Benefit Management Institute, 2013).

15. Bruce E. Landon et al., "Incentive Formularies and Changes in Prescription Drug Spending," *American Journal of Managed Care* 13, no. 6 (June 2007): 360–369.

16. Jon R. Gabel et al., "Withering on the Vine: The Decline of Indemnity Health Insurance," *Health Affairs* 19, no. 5 (September 2000): 152–157.

17. James C. Robinson, "Renewed Emphasis on Consumer Cost Sharing in Health Insurance Benefit Design," *Health Affairs* (March 2002), doi: 10.1377/hlthaff.w2.139.

18. Michael E. Chernew et al., "Value-Based Insurance Design," *Health Affairs* 26, no. 2 (March 2007): w195–w203.

19. Vanessa Fuhrmans, "A Radical Prescription," *Wall Street Journal,* May 10, 2004.

20. Matthew L. Maciejewski et al., "Copayment Reductions Generate Greater Medication Adherence in Targeted Patients," *Health Affairs* 29, no. 11 (November 2010): 2002–2008; *Aetna Launching Value-Based Program That Improves Medication Adherence, Cost and Outcomes for Members Who Have Suffered from Heart Attacks,* press release, November 14,

2011,www.aetna.com/news/newsReleases/2011/1114-AetnaRx-Healthy Outcomes.html.

21. US Department of Health & Human Services, *Preventive Services Covered under the Affordable Care Act,* www.hhs.gov/healthcare/facts /factsheets/2010/07/preventive-services-list.html.

22. James C. Robinson, "Applying Value-Based Insurance Design to High-Cost Health Services," *Health Affairs* 29, no. 11 (November 2010): 2009–2016.

23. Lynne Taylor, "80% of US Prescriptions Are Now Generic, Says IMS," *PharmaTimes,* August 3, 2012; Generic Pharmaceutical Association, *Generic Drug Savings in the U.S.* (Washington, DC: Generic Pharmaceutical Association, 2013).

24. David C. Grabowski et al., "The Large Social Value Resulting from Use of Statins Warrants Steps to Improve Adherence and Broader Treatment," *Health Affairs* 31, no. 10 (October 2012): 2276–2285.

25. Zitter Group, *Prior Authorization Tracking Tool for Rheumatoid Arthritis: Trends in the Marketplace* (San Francisco: Zitter Group, 2011).

26. Personal communication: Stan Mendenhall, Editor, Orthopedic Network News, May 7, 2013.

27. Tim Calkins. "Zimmer: The Gender Specific Knee," Northwestern University, Kellogg School of Management, Case KEL276, January 2007.

28. James C. Robinson and Kimberly MacPherson, "Payers Test Reference Pricing and Centers of Excellence to Steer Patients to Low-Price and High-Quality Providers," *Health Affairs* 31, no. 9 (September 2012): 2028–2036.

INDEX

copayment, 129–30, 132, 134–37, 149
cost effectiveness analysis (CEA),
  3, 9, 13, 43, 49–51, 58. *See also*
  Centers for Medicare and
  Medicaid Services (CMS)
cost sharing, 5, 9, 16–18, 56, 87, 120,
  125–27, 131–41, 146, 148–49, 152
coverage: criteria, 3, 7, 43–44;
  insurance coverage, 12–13, 17–18,
  24, 35, 41, 58; policy, 13, 17, 24,
  40–42, 47, 51–52, 58, 144–45
Coverage with Evidence Development (CED), 46–47, 58, 90. *See
  also* Centers for Medicare and
  Medicaid Services (CMS)

deductible, 127–28, 130–32, 134
defibrillator registry, 47
Diagnosis Related Group (DRG),
  64–65, 69, 76, 161n2
diagnostic test, 10, 34, 45, 52, 149
drug: development, 22, 63; formulary, 129; generic, 23, 60, 129–30,
  145, 151; regulatory framework
  for, 10–11, 19–26, 33–36, 39

efficacy, 6, 8–10, 13, 20–22, 25–27, 139,
  151
episode of care, 69. *See also*
  payment
European Medicines Agency
  (EMA), 33; regulatory approach,
  33–36
evidence-based: care, 13, 152;
  protocol, 10, 52, 77, 120, 144, 149
evidence dossier, 23

FDA: approval, 18, 20, 22–23, 29, 35,
  43, 76, 144; authorization, 13, 19,
  21–22, 35–36, 38, 75, 143, 151;
  regulatory framework, 21, 33,
  35–36; regulatory requirements,

19, 21–22, 28; review, 6, 26, 28–29,
  31, 142–43; postmarket or
  postlaunch surveillance, 18,
  20–21, 32, 36–38, 90, 142–43;
  premarket approval (PMA)
  pathway, 25–29, 32–33, 142; Risk
  Evaluation and Mitigation
  Strategies (REMS), 37; 510(k)
  premarket notification pathway,
  25, 27–30, 32–33, 142
fee for service, 14, 61, 63–65, 71, 74.
  See also payment
510(k) premarket notification
  pathway. *See* FDA
Fountain Valley Regional
  Hospital, 102, 103*table,* 106*table,*
  108–9, 111–12*table,* 113

health care expenditures, 2, 72, 65,
  74, 82, 85; growth of, 2, 65, 85
high-deductible health plan, 127.
  See also deductible
Hoag Memorial Presbyterian
  Hospital, 101–2
Hoag Orthopedic Institute (HOI),
  102, 103*table,* 106*table,* 111–12*table,*
  116, 118
hospital: as purchaser, 14–16, 18,
  79–99; competition, 56–57,
  81–82, 86; consolidation, 87;
  efficiency, 9, 15, 69, 75, 79, 96–98,
  105, 113–14, 116, 118; procurement,
  60, 78, 80, 87, 91–93, 105; quality
  improvement, 77, 96–97, 114;
  technology assessment, 9–10, 16,
  18, 60, 80, 84, 88–90, 95, 100–1,
  105, 108–9, 113, 146

implantable medical devices, 3,
  8–9, 14–15, 20–21, 24, 37, 61, 66, 71,
  81, 83, 85, 91, 105, 113, 121, 137–38,
  151; variance across hospitals in

physicians, 3, 5, 9–10, 13–15, 18–21, 23–24, 34, 37–38, 40, 44, 47–48, 52–53, 56, 58, 60, 62–65, 69, 71–73, 78–79, 81–84, 87–92, 96, 98, 100–3, 105, 107–9, 115–17, 120, 122–23, 125, 133, 136, 138, 141–43, 145–47, 151–52; brand preferences of, 83–84

PMA pathway. *See* FDA

PMA supplement. *See* FDA

premarket approval. *See* FDA

purchasing, 2, 3, 8–10, 12, 16, 18–21, 42, 61, 64, 71, 78, 80, 83, 96, 98; of medical technology, 3, 21, 42, 71, 78, 98, 101–2, 106, 109, 113, 133, 141, 146, 152; value-based, 8–10, 18, 141, 152

quality, 2, 5, 7–8, 14–15, 28, 38, 42–45, 55–57, 59, 61, 65, 69, 77, 79, 90, 94, 96–98, 113–14, 125, 129–31, 135

quality-adjusted life year, 50–51

readmissions, 56–57, 59, 68–69, 71, 77, 90, 98, 121, 148; readmission rates, 68

reasonable and necessary. *See* Medicare coverage policy

reference pricing, 130–31, 136, 138

regulatory barrier, 12

reimbursement, 5, 12, 17, 23, 42–44, 49–50, 52, 54, 57–63, 65, 69, 77–78, 85–86, 88–89, 95, 110, 111–12*table*, 145; volume-based, 63

relative value scales. *See* fee-for-service payment

risk, 7, 11–12, 19–22, 24–31, 33, 37, 39–40, 43–44, 48, 51–52, 70, 72–74, 94, 97, 117, 122–25, 128, 143, 145–47, 150; mitigation, 20

Risk Evaluation and Mitigation Strategies (REMS). *See* FDA

safety, 6, 9–10, 13, 20–22, 25–27, 30, 32–33, 36, 39, 46, 139, 143, 150

shared decision-making, 120, 122–25, 133

stent, 34–38, 45, 54, 68, 75–77, 83, 97; drug-eluting, 35–36, 38, 54, 76–77, 83

St. Joseph Health, 101–2, 105, 108, 113, 119

St. Jude Medical Center, 102, 103*table*, 105, 106–7*table*, 108–10, 111–12*table*, 113

substantial equivalence, 25, 27–28, 30, 33

surgery, 4, 7–8, 25–26, 30–31, 35, 38–39, 45, 53–54, 56–57, 59–61, 63–65, 68–69, 71–72, 75–76, 82, 85, 87, 104–5, 114–19, 121–25, 128–29, 135; orthopedic, 7, 30, 57, 72, 104, 118–19, 121–23; spine, 7, 103*table*, 104–5

surveillance, 12, 18, 20–21, 32, 36–38, 90, 142–43. *See also* FDA

TAVR, 4–5, 35, 38

Tenet Healthcare, 101–2

utilization management, 13, 53. *See also* medical management

value, 3, 5, 7–9, 13, 16–17, 24, 42, 62, 76, 93, 96, 120–21, 140, 147–48, 150; in medical technology, 3, 120, 140

value-based insurance design, 131–33, 137

value-based purchasing. *See* purchasing